ESSENTIALS
OF MASS
COMMUNICATION
THEORY

ESSENTIALS OF MASS COMMUNICATION THEORY

ARTHUR ASA BERGER

SAGE Publications
International Educational and Professional Publisher
Thousand Oaks   London   New Delhi

Copyright © 1995 by Sage Publications, Inc.

For information address:

SAGE Publications, Inc.
2455 Teller Road
Thousand Oaks, California 91320
E-mail: order@sagepub.com

SAGE Publications Ltd.
6 Bonhill Street
London EC2A 4PU
United Kingdom

SAGE Publications India Pvt. Ltd.
M-32 Market
Greater Kailash I
New Delhi 110 048 India

Printed in the United States of America

Library of Congress Cataloging-in-Publication Data

Berger, Arthur Asa, 1933-
   Essentials of mass communication theory / Arthur Asa Berger.
      p.   cm.
   Includes bibliographical references (p.   ) and index.
   ISBN 0-8039-7356-X.—ISBN 0-8039-7357-8 (pbk.)
      1. Mass media—Philosophy. 2. Mass media—United States.
   I. Title.
   P90.B413   1995
   302.23'0973—dc20   95-11882

This book is printed on acid-free paper.

   96 97 98 99 10 9 8 7 6 5 4 3 2

Sage Production Editor: Astrid Virding
Sage Typesetter: Andrea D. Swanson

CONTENTS

ACKNOWLEDGMENTS

I would like to thank my editor, Sophy Craze, for her support and help with this book. Two of my colleagues in the Broadcast and Electronic Communication Arts Department at San Francisco State University also deserve special mention. Ron Compesi went over the manuscript and listed a number of topics that needed attention. Chaim Eyal, in a really remarkable display of collegiality and command of the subject, took my diskette for the first draft of this book and wrote a number of comments on it, some quite lengthy, about various topics—many of which I have included in the manuscript as personal correspondence. I have also benefited from the support of my colleagues in the Broadcast and Electronic Communication Arts Department, and from our discussions, over the years, about media, mass communication, and related matters. I was fortunate enough to be awarded a leave with pay to work on this book, and appreciate the support of San Francisco State University to do this.

I was a visiting professor at the Annenberg School for Communication at the University of Southern California during the 1984-1985 academic year, and I gained a great deal from that experience (though I found living in Los Angeles traumatic). A considerable number of scholars visited the school to give lectures, and there was a good deal of intellectual ferment. The Annenberg School also hosted a number of conferences on various aspects of communication in the early 1980s that I found extremely useful. I am grateful to Peter Clarke, who was the dean then (and who explained to me that I was "data free"), for inviting me to spend a year there and to the faculty of the Annenberg School, in particular Elihu Katz, Daniel Dayan, Bill Dutton, and Mike Noll.

I have also benefited from the work of a number of mass communication and mass media scholars, some of whose publications are listed in the reference section of this book. I have had the pleasure of meeting and talking about mass communication, popular culture, and related topics with scholars from many different countries in recent years, and these meetings and conversations (as well as letters and e-mail in some cases) have been of great benefit.

I want to express my appreciation to the following people: Kim Schröder of the University of Roskilde, Hyeon Dew Kang of Seoul National University, Tain-Dow Lee of Fu Jen Catholic University in Taipei, Darunee Hirunrak of Chulalongkorn University in Bangkok, Klaus Bruhn Jensen of the University of Copenhagen, Karl Erik Rosengren of Lund University, Steen Sauerberg of the University of Copenhagen, Bo Reimer of the University of Gothenburg, Michel Danesi of the University of Toronto, Irving Louis Horowitz of Rutgers University, the late Aaron Wildavsky of the University of California at Berkeley, and William Fry of Stanford University. I would also like to thank Sage Publications production editor Astrid Virding and copy editor Judy Selhorst for their assistance with this project.

As Flaubert put it with aphoristic bitterness, 1789 had destroyed the aristocracy, 1848 the bourgeoisie, and 1851, the people. Now only the mob remained. Stendhal attributed the presence of mass attitudes to the big cities and dependence of their inhabitants upon impersonal means of communication. It was not only that the size of the community kept men from appropriating social experience first-hand. A habit of social distance and indirection had actually developed, even toward events which occurred within reach so that, as Stendhal said, a man going by a house where something unusual had happened would rather wait for the account of next day's newspapers than to look in the window. The fundamental difference between Paris and a village was that the village trusted that it could understand its life directly, whereas Paris saw everything "through the dailies."

César Graña, *Modernity and Its Discontents*, 1967

CHAPTER 1

MAKING SENSE OF
MASS COMMUNICATION

This introductory chapter begins with a number of scenarios describing possible readers of this book and their involvement with various aspects of the mass media and mass communication. I suggest that there are five focal points—basic areas of concern—that we might consider in dealing with the mass media: artworks or texts (which are the content of the media), artists (who create works carried by the media), audiences (who read, listen to, and see mass-mediated works), America or society (where the audiences are found), and a medium (which not only carries texts but affects them). It is possible, I point out, to deal with these focal points or areas singly or in various combinations. I then define the terms *mass* and *communication* and deal with a number of the more important levels and models of the communication process. I conclude with a discussion of some controversies in mass communication theory and distinguish among theories, concepts, and the applications of concepts and theories.

Let's start this book about **mass communication** with you, the reader. I will project a number of scenarios about possible readers that describe who they might be and what they might be doing or might have done. One of these scenarios might contain elements that are similar to the ways you, or one of your friends, use the mass media.

Some Scenarios

Scenario 1. It is late in the evening in Chicago (or wherever you might live in the U.S.A.) and you are listening to your favorite "pop classics" station on the radio, station KPOP. Johnny Mathis (or whichever singer you like) is singing "It's All in the Game" (or any song you like). The station you choose to listen to, and the songs that station broadcasts, is affected by your age, education, race, sex, friends, and a host of other things.

Radio stations **narrowcast**; that is, they direct their programs to relatively narrow segments of the general population. If you are listening to a light rock station, chances are you are over 30—or over 40. If you are listening to a pop classics station, you might be over 50. If you are listening to hard rock, you might be in your late teens or early 20s. You may be listening to a station that plays songs by Madonna or plays rap music or country western or is all talk shows. In a major market, such as the San Francisco area, there are more than 60 radio stations, so there is something for everyone.

Scenario 2. It is 7:00 a.m. in San Francisco and you are watching the *Today* show (or one of its competitors) on your television set. Why you watch one morning program, such as *Today*, rather than one on a different network is a subject of consuming interest to television executives and advertisers. Is it because you like the hosts on one show better than those on others? Or do you intensely dislike one or more of the hosts on the shows you don't watch?

Scenario 3. It is midnight. You aren't sleepy or can't sleep, so you are listening to a CD of Chopin's piano music played by Vladimir Horowitz. While you listen to the music, you are reading Ernest Hemingway's *The Sun Also Rises*. You could be listening to a different CD and reading a different book. Your choice of music, the books you read—these things are connected to your age, education, gender, social class, aesthetic sensibilities, occupation, and what sociologists

While critics in the humanities have grown more and more bold in proclaiming the reader's power over the images on a printed page or celluloid strip, few have paid much attention to the emergence of new media that call into question the very categories of author, reader, and text.... Interactive software—computer games, hypertext, and even "desktop" programs and databases—connect the oppositions of "reader" and "text," of "reading" and "writing," together in feedback loops that make it impossible to distinguish precisely where one begins and the other ends. Recognizing a reader's changing expectations and reactions as a linear text unfolds is one thing, but how do we talk about textual interactions in which every response provokes instantaneous changes in the text itself, leading to a new response, and so on. The answer is not very clear yet, for whereas the humanities have theoretical accounts to explain the workings of literature, film, and television, as yet there is no "software theory."

Ted Friedman, "Making Sense of Software," 1995, p. 73

would describe as your **lifestyle**. Why some people like "classic" novels and others like "trashy" romances is a matter of interest to people in the publishing industry, authors, and those who study mass communication.

Let's consider the above scenarios analytically. What we find is that each of them involves

1. someone who can be seen as a member of an **audience,**
2. who is involved with a program or a book (a **text**),
3. created by some writer or performer or collection of **artists** and performers,
4. that involves some **medium** (radio, television, CDs, books),
5. that is taking place somewhere in **America**.

This list calls attention to what I refer to here as the **focal points** of mass communication and the mass media, major topics of interest that we can consider. In this book I devote a chapter to each of these focal points. There are other ways of dealing with the topics to be considered in a book on mass communication, but I feel this list of focal points provides a pretty good way of covering the most important topics.

Focal Points in Mass Communication

I want to offer here a mnemonic (that is, easy to keep in mind) device that will help you remember the focal points: Except for the matter of the media, they all start with *A*. Let's consider these focal points as they apply to our first scenario, involving the person listening to "It's All in the Game."

Artwork. The song (or, to use the term critics prefer, the text) our first reader is listening to, "It's All in the Game," is an example of a work of art—in this case, popular or mass art. The term **popular,** as we will see, is the subject of considerable confusion and the source of many debates among mass communication scholars. The song suggests that love is "a game," a **metaphor** that has a number of notions that follow from it: Someone wins and someone loses, there is strategy involved, some players cheat, there are rules, and so on. Works of art, or texts, entertain us, but they do other things as well.

Audience. The hero or heroine of our first scenario and the others who are listening to that song on that radio station are members of that particular station's audience and listen to it because its disk jockeys play the kind of music the audience members like.

Medium. We are talking here about radio, but there are many media that are the instruments of mass communication in society, including television, film, books, magazines, newspapers, records, video games, computers, and CD-ROM.

America (society). In the first scenario, the hero or heroine lives in Chicago and thus in the United States of America. The discussions in

Figure 1.1. Focal Points in Mass Communication

this volume are not always limited to America, but deal with society in general and the social aspects of mass communication and the mass media. I use America (rather than United States) in my discussion to keep the alliteration: Four *A*'s and an *M* make it easy to remember the focal points.

Artist (creator). Every text is created by some artist or writer or some member of a team in collaborative media, such as film and television. CDs and videos and video games are complex works that involve all kinds of people: performers, writers of songs and scripts, technicians, and musicians, to name some of the most important ones. And now, with the development of CD-ROMs, we have interactive media that allow individuals to "participate," although in limited ways, in the construction of texts, to insinuate themselves into various adventures, to play all kinds of roles and do all kinds of other things.

The five focal points to be considered in our discussion of mass communications, and their relations to one another, are shown in Figure 1.1. We can also deal with each of these five focal points on its own; some of the topics we might consider in doing so are shown in Table 1.1. In Figure 1.1, arrows connect the five focal points in various ways, showing that we can consider such relationships as the following:

1. that between artwork and artist (AB)
2. that between artwork and medium (AC)
3. that between artwork and audience (AD)
4. that between artwork and American society (AE)
5. that between artist and medium (BC)
6. that between artist and audience (BD)
7. that between artist and American society (BE)
8. that between medium and audience (CD)

TABLE 1.1 Focal Points and Selected Topics of Analysis

Artwork	Audience	America	Artist	Medium
critical techniques	cultures and subcultures	social functions of mass communication	kinds of artists	transportation theories
content analysis	uses and gratifications	criticism of mass media	artists as encoders	responsive chord theories
texts	functionalism	postmodernism	images of artists	McLuhan's ideas
genres	decoding	critical research	intention and art	media effects
popular culture	political cultures	administrative research	psychology of creation	ownership of mass media
mass culture	segmentation		auteur theory	violence
intertextuality	taste			media aesthetics

  9. that between medium and American society (CE)
 10. that between audience and American society (DE)

We can also deal with three of the focal points at the same time as well (ABC, BCD, CDE), but let me suggest that would needlessly complicate matters. Using the five focal points as a means of organizing this book, we can discuss a large number of topics. As you read the material that is to follow, it would be useful for you to consider whether I am dealing primarily with one of the focal points on its own or, if not, which relationships I am addressing. In many cases I deal with topics that involve several focal points; in the same light, it is difficult in some places to insist that a given topic should be treated under one focal point rather than another, because the concerns involved are so complicated. I place my discussions of particular topics where I think they fit most logically.

You will see, as you read this book, that arguments about mass communication, mass media, audiences, masses, and related matters have been going on for something like 50 years now, and many of the early negative arguments are still being made, just as many of the defenses of the mass media, popular culture, the public arts, and so on, go back to the 1930s and 1940s as well.

We must also keep in mind the dimension of time. Each of the elements in Figure 1.1 takes place at a certain point in time: Someone writes a television script, it is produced, and then it is broadcast to people who tune in, at a certain point in time, to see it. We must be mindful of the time element, especially as it relates to certain media— the way different television networks schedule and counterschedule programs, for instance. We also have to consider the matter of trends and changes in audience tastes.

Defining Our Terms: Mass

We generally make a distinction between the process of *mass communication*, in which information (or texts) is disseminated to large numbers of people, the so-called masses, and the *mass media*, which are the means of carrying or communicating this material to these people. More than 40 years ago, Eliot Friedson (1953) wrote:

> In the dictionary the mass is defined as the great body of the people of a nation, as contrasted to some special body like a particular social class. Lazarsfeld and Kendall use such a definition when they write "The term 'mass' then, is truly applicable to the medium of radio, for it more than the other media, reaches all groups of the population uniformly." This notion of the mass merely implies that a mass communication may be distinguished from other kinds of communication by the fact that it is addressed to a large cross-section of a population rather than only one or a few individuals or a special part of the population. It also makes the implicit assumption of some technical means of transmitting the communication in order that the communication may reach at the same time all the people forming the cross-section of the population. (p. 313)

Friedson argues that this definition is inadequate. He moves on to a second interpretation of the term **mass** that lists four basic characteristics:

1. It is heterogeneous, with members coming from a wide variety of groups in society.
2. The individuals in this mass do not know one another.
3. The members of this mass are separated from one another and cannot interact with one another or exchange their experiences with one another.

4. There is no leadership to the mass and there is a very loose organization to it, if there is any organization at all.

He offers a quote from a distinguished sociologist, Herbert Blumer (1936), who wrote criticisms that are typical of the thinking of many sociologists of the time (and still now) relative to the **concept** of "the mass":

[The mass] has no social organization, no body of customs and tradition, no established set of rules or rituals, no organized group of sentiments, no structure or status roles, and no established leadership. It merely consists of an aggregation of individuals who are separate, detached, anonymous. (in Friedson, 1953, p. 314)

This list of characteristics of the mass is also used to describe what some call our *mass society* and *mass culture*.

Friedson attacks these notions by suggesting that they are not based on facts. He offers the example of moviegoing, which he points out is often a group-based activity. In addition, he reminds us that the most effective kind of advertising is word-of-mouth, which suggests that members of audiences are not as separated from one another as "mass" theorists would have us believe. Friedson also discusses **opinion leader** theory, which posits that people, as members of small groups, are exposed to the opinions of their group leaders and can be affected by them. This **theory** would suggest that people are not as alienated as Blumer and others like him have suggested.

The term *mass* has negative connotations in American society, as in most societies. It suggests a crowd, a huge number of people who are easily manipulated by demagogues, a group of people who are alienated from one another and can be dangerous in certain situations. In terms of mass communication, the term suggests that aside from living in the United States, Americans have only the text on the medium they are listening to (Johnny Mathis singing "All in the Game" on a radio station) in common.

Individualism and the Mass Media

As Americans, we tend to pride ourselves on being individualists, and the notion that we are members of some undifferentiated mass of people bothers us. One reason it should bother us is because it probably is incorrect. A great deal of the thinking about "the mass" comes from European social theorists who were transplanted to the United States and reacted, negatively, to the egalitarian society in which they found themselves and the level of culture they found here. What these sociologists, such as Blumer and others, have written about the masses is similar in certain respects to the work of Gustave Le Bon (1895/1960), who wrote a work titled *The Crowd*. Le Bon's crowds became, without too much modification, Blumer's (and others') masses.

The term *individualism* was coined by Alexis de Tocqueville in the 19th century. He warned us that our individualism could become excessive and lead to a state of anarchy, but he also pointed out that Americans are inveterate joiners, members of many voluntary associations. We have to be careful, then, when we think about *mass*, for it may suggest things about ourselves and American society that are somewhat removed from reality. As Friedson notes (and remember, this article was written in 1953):

> There is no justification for studying the audience as an aggregation of discrete individuals whose social experience is equalized and cancelled out by means of allowing only the attributes of age, sex, socio-economic status, and the like, to represent them except by subscribing to the assertion that the audience is a mass. (p. 316)

We can see this in the radio industry, for, as I have noted above, radio is a mass medium that now is characterized by extreme narrowcasting. In the San Francisco Bay Area, for example, there are more than 60 radio stations catering to an incredible variety of tastes—each station seeking its segment of the audience in the area. Narrowcasting is now found in television also, with some channels devoted to a single genre—such as music, comedy, or news.

There is another meaning of *mass* that should be mentioned, and that concerns the matter of the communication itself, which is transmitted to large numbers of people by one or another medium. The focus here is on the communication itself, and not on the audience. The designation of *mass* in this case refers to messages intended for large groups of people and disseminated by one of the media, as contrasted with a singular message, as in a letter or telephone conversation. Television shows, for example, are typically received by many sets, depending on the nature of the program being disseminated. An interesting question arises: If a television program is broadcast but only one person in the whole country watches it, is the process of mass communication going on?

Defining Our Terms: Communication

Communication has, as its root, the word *community*, for good reason. Communities are held together by communication, and it is through this process that culture is passed on from one generation to the next. The term *communication* generally is held to involve some kind of a transfer of information from one person to another or to a group of other people. **Communications**, on the other hand, refers not to the process but to the messages transmitted. (In academic circles, there is some disagreement about whether the field is *communication* or *communications*, and there are some departments, schools, and colleges of communication and others of communications. I will generally use the singular; the whole controversy really is a tempest in a teapot.)

The transmission of information in communication, according to Claude Shannon, a pioneer in information theory, must contain some element of uncertainty about what the source of the message will produce (cited in Pierce & Noll, 1990, pp. 54-65). For example, if you

know what a person is going to say before she says it, she has not, technically speaking, conveyed information. There are, let me point out, many different theories about what communication is and how we gain information. I discuss a number of these in this volume.

The terms *communication* and *community* share the same Latin root as the word *common—communis.* This common denominator is important to the understanding of the process of communication on two levels. First, the quality of the communication process is understood to be higher among participants who have certain things in common, such as past experiences, values, and beliefs. These are also attributes of a community of individuals. Second, the process of communication, mass or otherwise, requires encoding (by a sender) and decoding (by a receiver), which can be achieved successfully only by participants who share a common set of codes—that is, language.

Levels of Communication

We can distinguish among a number of kinds or levels of communication, including intrapersonal, interpersonal, small group, and mass communication.

Intrapersonal communication. Intrapersonal communication is the internal or intrapsychic dialogue that often takes place in our heads, what commonly is referred to as "talking to oneself." We do not usually actually talk aloud to ourselves; rather, we think about things, carrying on internal dialogues. The content or text of intrapersonal communication consists of thoughts. The medium or channel of this kind of communication is the neurological/chemical apparatus through which thoughts are processed in the brain. (Dreams fit into this category also.)

Interpersonal communication. Interpersonal communication takes place between a person and someone else or some others in a relatively small collection of people. Sometimes the communicators are acquainted, as at a dinner party, and sometimes they are not, as when strangers speak on the street, on a bus, or in a supermarket. The medium here is the airwaves, and the text is what is said and how it is said. A great deal is also communicated by nonverbal means—through body language, facial expression, clothes, and so on.

Small group communication. Small group communication involves a considerable number of people, such as when a person gives a lecture in a class or a speech to a gathering of people. We also use language and talk here as well as various kinds of **nonverbal communication.**

Mass communication. Mass communication involves the use of print or electronic media, such as newspapers, magazines, film, radio, or television, to communicate to large numbers of people who are located in various places—often scattered all over the country or world. The people reached may be in groups of varying sizes or may be lone individuals. A number of different elements make up mass communications media; images, spoken language, printed language, sound effects, music, color, lighting, and a variety of other techniques are used to communicate messages and obtain particular effects.

Although I have separated the mass media from the process of mass communication in the discussion above, some people tie them together and talk about the "mass media of communication." The two are closely linked, though I will continue to separate them, reserving the term *mass media* for the instruments by which mass communication is achieved.

Lasswell's Communication Model

Many different communication **models** have been created by scholars in a number of different disciplines. A model, for purposes of this discussion, is a highly abstract representation of what goes on in the real world. It is abstract because it must be able to cover a large number of different possibilities. We use models because they enable to us to understand complicated matters by separating them into their components and seeing how they function.

Denis McQuail and Sven Windahl's book *Communication Models* (1993) lists a good number of such models. It starts off with one of

TABLE 1.2 Lasswell's Theory and the Focal Points

Who?	artist
Says what?	artwork or text
In which channel?	medium
To whom?	audience
With what effect?	society (impact on)

the most famous, one elaborated by a political scientist, Harold Lasswell, in 1948. McQuail and Windahl quote what they describe as "perhaps the most famous single phrase in communication research"—what has become known as the *Lasswell formula* (p. 13):

Who?
Says what?
In which channel?
To whom?
With what effect?

We can see that this formula deals with a number of the focal points discussed above (see Table 1.2). Figure 1.1 does not deal with the matter of *effects* directly, but in directing our attention to audiences and to society in general, it implicitly takes the matter of effects into consideration.

McQuail and Windahl (1993) point out that Lasswell's inclusion of effects in his model is problematic:

> The Lasswell Formula shows a typical trait of early communication models: it more or less takes for granted that the communicator has some intention of influencing the receiver and, hence, that communication should be treated mainly as a persuasive process. It is also assumed that messages always have effects. Models such as this have surely contributed to the tendency to exaggerate the effects of, especially, mass communication. (p. 14)

They also point out that like many other early theorists, Lasswell did not consider the matter of feedback; his model is unidirectional, going from someone who says something to someone who receives a message and is affected by it.

Gerbner's Model of Communication

George Gerbner has developed a model somewhat like Lasswell's, which I would like to mention in passing:

1. Someone
2. perceives an event
3. and reacts
4. in a situation
5. through some means
6. to make available materials
7. in some form
8. and context
9. conveying content
10. with some consequence.

Gerbner has also developed some complicated diagrams to show his model in operation. He expands upon the Lasswell formula, focusing attention on perception and reaction by the perceiver and the consequences of the communication (for further discussion of Gerbner's model, see McQuail & Windahl, 1993, pp. 23-26).

Let us consider now another model that will help us to understand the communication process—one developed by Roman Jakobson, a distinguished linguist who looks at communication from a somewhat different perspective.

Jakobson's Model of the Communication Process

Jakobson's model, shown in Figure 1.2, works as follows. A sender or speaker sends a message to someone, a receiver. The message is delivered by a *code* (such as the English language and the way it is used) via a contact (medium) such as speech. The context in which a message is found generally helps us make sense of the message. For example, the words "Hand me the hypodermic syringe" mean one thing when spoken in a hospital and another when said in a dark alley. We cannot equate a message with the meaning someone gets from the message; the two are sometimes quite different, because

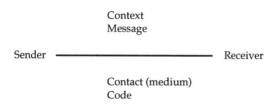

Figure 1.2. Jakobson's Six Elements of a Speech Act

meaning is connected to the entire speech event and is affected by context and the contact (see Jakobson, 1988).

Robert Sholes (1974) discusses Jakobson's model:

> Whether we are considering ordinary conversation, a public speech, a letter, or a poem, we always find a *message* which proceeds from a *sender* to a *receiver*. These are the most obvious aspects of communication. But a successful communication depends on three other aspects of the event as well: the message must be delivered through a *contact*, physical and/or psychological; it must be framed in a *code*; and it must refer to a *context*. In the area of context, we find what a message is about. But to get there we must understand the code in which the message is framed—as in the present case, my messages reach you through the medium of an academic/literary subcode of the English language. And even if we have the code, we understand nothing until we make contact with the utterance; in the present case, until you see the printed words on this page (or hear them read aloud) they do not exist as a message for you. The message itself, uniting sender and receiver, in the quintessentially human act of communication, is simply a verbal form, which depends on all the other elements of a speech event to convey its meaning. *The message is not the meaning.* Meaning lies at the end of the speech event, which gives the verbal formula its life and color. (p. 24)

As Sholes points out, the process of communication is complicated; it is not to be equated with simply sending a message.

Messages, according to Jakobson, have a number of functions. The most common is the **referential function,** which relates to the surroundings in which the speaker finds him- or herself. But messages also have **emotive functions,** expressing the feelings of the sender, and **poetic functions,** which involve the use of literary devices, such as metaphors, similes, and word choices, to give a message its tone and distinctive qualities (or voice).

Speech events, and by implication communication in general, as Jakobson's model shows, are complicated matters that involve a number of different phenomena. Jakobson's model, like all models, has problems; for instance, we don't know whether his term *message* applies to the words uttered or to the meaning of the words uttered. Nevertheless, the model is useful in that it offers a good overview of the communication process.

We can also expand the concept of message to include nonverbal communication, or "signs," such as body language, hair color, facial expression, clothes, props (eyeglasses, rings), and status symbols (such as mansions or "trophy wives"). We are always sending messages, whether we realize it or not. How people "read" these messages, including the ones we don't realize we are sending, is a subject of considerable importance. It is not too much of an exaggeration to suggest that not only are we always sending messages to others, but others are always sending messages to us, even if nobody says a word. And not saying a word, in certain circumstances, is also a message—such as when someone asks, "How are you?" or "Do you love me?"

The Osgood-Schramm Circular Model

I have raised above the matter of feedback—of the ways people respond to messages and communications of various kinds. One very well known model that deals with feedback, the Osgood and Schramm circular model, focuses attention on the individuals involved in the communication process (see Figure 1.3). In this model, we see that message senders also are message receivers. *Encoding* here is understood to mean putting information into a form that can be understood and sending a message; *decoding* refers to receiving the encoded message and interpreting it. For example, we can take a thought, encode it in English, and say something to someone, who then decodes the words and understands (to some extent) what was said. McQuail and Windahl (1993) describe the importance of this model:

> The emergence of this approach meant a clear break with the traditional linear/one-way picture of communication. The model is especially useful in describing interpersonal communication but is less suitable

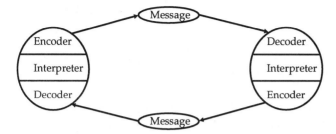

Figure 1.3. Osgood and Schramm's Circular Model

for cases without, or with little feedback. Mass communication is such a case. (p. 20)

They point out that in his later work Schramm modified his theories in order to address mass communication.

The Sapir-Whorf Hypothesis and Its Implications for Media Study

I would like to call attention to an important aspect of communication, namely, the language we use. The words we use affect the messages we send and shape, in part, the responses people give to our messages as well as people's perceptions of their society and the world itself. This notion, that language is not merely a transparent means of delivering information or messages, is generally known as the **Sapir-Whorf hypothesis,** after two famous linguists, Edward Sapir and Benjamin Lee Whorf, who elaborated it many years ago. As Sapir (1929) has written:

The relation between language and experience is often misunderstood. Language is not a more or less systematic inventory of the various items of experience which seem relevant to the individual, as is so often naively assumed, but is also a self-contained, creative symbolic organization, which not only refers to experience largely acquired without its help but actually defines experience for us by reason of its formal completeness and because of our unconscious projection of its implicit expectations into the field of experience. . . . Such categories as number, gender, case, tense, mode, voice, "aspect" and a host of others, many of which are not recognized . . . are, of course derivative of experience at last analysis, but, once abstracted from experience, they are systematically elaborated in language and are not so much discovered in experience as imposed upon it because of the tyrannical hold that linguistic form has upon our orientation in the world.

The Sapir-Whorf **hypothesis** gives language a dominant role in shaping our perceptions of the world. Our language, it suggests, is a kind of prism that we use to make sense of the world; it is not a window pane that we can see through without any distortions, and it is not a mirror that reflects the world in which we live.

The language conventions we learn as we grow up in particular families in specific strata of society in given countries affect us in profound ways. What we know of society and the world, and what we think about them, is tied to the language habits of the group in which we find ourselves. We are, after all, social animals, and our ideas are, to a considerable extent, related to our social and economic circumstances. This notion can be pushed further, to suggest that different languages generate, so to speak, different worlds. As Sapir (1929) puts it, "The worlds in which different societies live are distinct worlds, not merely the same world with different labels attached." Language becomes, then, a central factor in our lives.

In the United States there are numerous accents and regionalisms, and various kinds of dialects and sublanguages. All of these variations on mainstream English generate different realities for their speakers. It has been said that England and America are two countries separated by a common language, but the same can be said about different groups in America that speak different kinds of English.

I would like to suggest (and I will develop this notion in more detail in Chapter 3) that the electronic and visual media also are not simply channels, or means of transporting messages. The media, which enable artists and creative personalities to control such things as lighting, sound, cutting, shot sequences, and other aspects of auditory and visual language (and also regular language) profoundly shape the messages we get from them. Marshall McLuhan (1965), a Canadian media theorist, actually went so far as to collapse the message into the medium and to argue that "the medium is the message." He believed that the conventions of the media are what is important, not the information, data, whatever, that the media disseminate. This position is a bit extreme, but it is reasonable to suggest that the media play a major role in shaping the messages they convey; they are not simply conduits that have no significant role. Where to draw the line between the medium and its messages is often hard to say.

The Play Theory of Mass Communication

There are many theories of communication and mass communication that I could discuss here, but let me conclude this brief examination with a theory that is much less abstract than Jakobson's theory of communication, one that offers some offbeat and interesting ideas. In 1967, William Stephenson published *The Play Theory of Mass Communication*, in which he suggests that the most significant function of mass communication is to facilitate "subjective play," to give people pleasure, an interlude from the pressing matters that concern them most of the time. Stephenson sees mass communication as serving two functions. The first is to provide play, to influence customs, normalize manners, give people something in common to talk about, so as to foster mutual socialization. The second function is to help shake up society:

> The other purpose of mass communication is to "rock the boat," to be in the forefront of change in status quo conditions. The press, traditionally, has served revolution and revolt. It is important to notice that it is difficult to change basic beliefs, though in a revolution that is perhaps exactly what happens willy-nilly. It takes a cataclysmic event, however, to bring this about. The achievement of mass communication lies in the way it short-circuits older beliefs, substituting new values for them. (Stephenson, 1967/1988, p. 65)

Stephenson distinguishes between **social controls** and **convergent selective conditions.** Social controls are tied to "deeply internalized beliefs which are difficult, if not impossible, to change" (p. 65). Convergent conditions, on the other hand, are about relatively trivial matters, such as what kind of soda pop one likes. Mass communication has, by implication, a very difficult time changing basic beliefs, but it can play a role in shaping our convergent or momentary desires and the many relatively unimportant decisions we make. As Stephenson notes on the first page of his book:

> What, then, can mass communication do? It is the thesis of this book that at its best mass communication allows people to become absorbed in *subjective play.* . . . There are some who look with an uneasy eye at these mass pleasures; behind them they see the lurkings of "hidden persuasion" and "tyranny over the mind" (a view expressed by Aldous Huxley). Mankind, these critics feel, is being painlessly put to sleep by the cunning of advertisers and purveyors of mass pap for the public. This, it seems to me, is a jaundiced view.

Where many critics of mass communication have gone wrong, Stephenson asserts, is in studying it as essentially an agent of persuasion rather than as an agent of entertainment and pleasure. These scholars have been blind to the "play" aspects of mass communication—a shortcoming that Stephenson rectifies in his book.

In the introduction to a recent edition of *The Play Theory of Mass Communication,* Brian Sutton-Smith (1988) argues that Stephenson's theory has been relatively neglected by communication scholars because of their reliance on **functional** approaches to media (that is, the role the media play in stabilizing or destabilizing society) and their inability to take seriously and deal with something that seems as frivolous as play.

A Note on Controversies

In the field of mass communication, as in many other areas of academic life, many controversies exist. Of particular note are those concerning differing ideas among scholars about how to define *mass*, about which are the best models for understanding the communication process, about how one should study mass communication, about what effects the media of mass communication have, and about the role of media in society. We find the same kind of thing in the field of history, for example. Historians do not write about what happened in the past; rather, they offer interpretations about what happened. These interpretations are, ultimately, based on the interests of the historians and the methodologies they favor. Some historians are Marxists, some use psychoanalytic concepts, some use data and statistics, some focus on great figures, some focus on everyday life and the common people.

Thus in my discussion of Stephenson's play theory I have mentioned his observation that the focus in mass communication studies has been on the way mass communication affects people's **attitudes** and not on its aesthetic aspects. Much mass communication research is done by social psychologists who are interested in how mass communication shapes attitudes and opinions; they are not interested in what Stephenson describes as aesthetic considerations. Other scholars, from more humanistic disciplines, focus on such matters as the way mass communication transmits **culture,** the formulaic aspects of the texts found in the mass media, and the way these texts and the **aesthetic** aspects of the media that carry them generate meaning in people.

Over the years, different theories of mass communication have gained popularity and then faded into the background, as other theories and methods of studying mass communication have gained the spotlight. Some theorists believe that mass communication has powerful effects and have come up with a number of notions concerning these, such as that the media set our agendas for us, give us biased notions about reality (**cultivation theory**), or lead to a spiral of silence that dissuades people from voicing opposition to what they believe are widely accepted views. Other theorists believe that the effects of mass communication are weak or have **limited effects** and argue that research has not been able to prove powerful media effects.

Are Media Effects Weak or Powerful?

Concerning media effects, William J. McGuire (1991) has written:

> Although the general public and the diverse groups who are professionally involved with the media may be convinced that the mass media have vast direct impacts on the public, a considerable amount of empirical research on the topic has provided surprisingly little support for massive impact. Rather, the interim bottom line to which the existing research findings add up is that media effects can occasionally be detected statistically but are usually quite small in magnitude. (p. 279)

McGuire points out that methodological weaknesses, environmental conditions, and the search for general effects, which may lead to the neglect of circumscribed effects, all may contribute to our not having evidence of powerful media effects.

The notion of limited effects is not supported by everyone, however. As Chaim Eyal (personal communication, 1994) has noted:

> The limited effects notions are conceptualizations of the past. Very few, if any, theoreticians cling to those ideas. In the first place, the notion of null, or limited, effects originated from a very narrow line of research—the impact of political campaigns, studies in the late 1940s and early 1950s. Not much later it was recognized effects are not only in the realm of behavior but also in the area of cognition: awareness, knowledge, opinions, etc. With this recognition, which paralleled the development of the concept of attitudes by social psychologists, came the recognition that the mass media do have an impact—indeed different types of impact—in specific areas of people's thoughts, information processing, and life in general.

Still other mass communication scholars focus on the uses audiences make of media and the gratifications they get from them, not on the effects the media have on people.

There are good reasons to support each of the theories discussed above (which is why some scholars do support them), but there are also reasons to question their validity (which is why some scholars hold opposing or alternative views). You should recognize, then, that in the field of mass communication, as in most areas of scholarship where there is life and vitality, there is a great deal of ferment and argumentation going on.

Scholarly Disputes in the Study of Mass Communication

Scholars do not generally argue by calling one another names, though this happens from time to time. Instead, they do research and conduct experiments and write articles and books to support their hypotheses and test various propositions that, they believe, best describe and explain things. In this book you will find a number of ideas and concepts and theories that deal with a number of different aspects of mass communication and the mass media. Many of these ideas are quite ingenious and very persuasive. You will have to decide, in the final analysis, which of them you think most logical, most reasonable, most suggestive. So your role, as a reader, will have to be an active one, as you consider which perspectives explain things best, cover the most ground, and allow you to understand and interpret mass communication and the mass media in the most interesting and useful ways.

A Note on Terms and Definitions

At this point I would like to offer definitions of some of the general terms I use throughout this book (many more terms, in addition to those addressed here, are defined in the glossary; terms included in the glossary appear in boldface in the text on first mention). There is a good deal of disagreement among scholars here, too, about how to define terms, so it might be best to think of the definitions and explanations that follow as "working" ones.

We make sense of the world, at the most immediate level, by using **concepts**. Concepts can be thought of as ideas that help us to understand phenomena; they are the building blocks of our thinking. As George Lakoff and Mark Johnson (1980) note:

> The concepts that govern our thought are not just matters of the intellect. They also govern our everyday functioning, down to the most mundane details. Our concepts structure what we perceive, how we get around in the world, and how we relate to other people. Our conceptual system thus plays a central role in defining our everyday realities. If we are right in suggesting that our conceptual system is

largely metaphorical, then the way we think, what we experience, and
what we do every day is very much a matter of metaphor. (p. 3)

The essential thing about metaphors, they add, is that they allow us
to understand and experience "one thing in terms of another" (p. 5).
Human thought processes, according to Lakoff and Johnson, are
basically metaphoric, in that metaphors are at the heart of the concepts we use to make sense of the world.

Concepts and propositions are generally understood to be the
basic elements of **theories**. John Brewer and Albert Hunter (1989)
explain these relationships as follows:

> Concepts and propositions are a theory's chief components. The con-
> cepts define the phenomena being investigated. The propositions tell
> how and under what circumstances those conceptually defined phe-
> nomena are thought to be related. Theories logically explain, and also
> predict, empirical generalizations. (p. 32)

Theories, Brewer and Hunter suggest, are abstract ideas that are not
tied to any particular events and instances. Because they are so
abstract, we can generate many different theories to explain a particular phenomenon or some empirical data. Because the human
mind is so ingenious at thinking up theories, we need empirical
research to justify our theories, and even when we do have data that
seem to support a given theory there can be problems. Further, some
theories don't lend themselves to testing at all.

Let me, at the risk of oversimplifying, try to make sense of this
discussion of terms by suggesting that we have various levels to
consider. At the highest level we have some area of interest—the
mind, society, politics. The next level involves theories that try to
explain some aspect of the subject area. At a level below the theories
we have concepts and propositions, which are part of the theories.
At a level below this, we have behavior or applications—things that
happen in everyday life that the concepts and propositions explain.
Table 1.3 offers some examples.

Concepts and propositions are relational. Words have meaning,
but they do not convey information or ideas in themselves. They have
to be linked together, one way or another. And we must remember

TABLE 1.3 Theories, Concepts, and Applications

Theory	*Concept*	*Application*
Psychoanalytic	narcissism	person who loves self
Marxist	ideology	belief system of ruling class
Gatekeeper	selectivity	those who determine what will be carried on news, etc.

that the meanings words have are the meanings we give them. It is only when we establish relationships that we have propositions and concepts.

In the chapters that follow, you will encounter a number of theories and concepts (sometimes it is hard to determine which is which) that scholars have used to explain how mass communication functions and how it affects individuals and societies. You will find that many different theories have been put forward, often to explain the same phenomena. It is the clash over theories that makes the subject of mass communication research so exciting. Why a person accepts one theory or methodology rather than another is a question that is intriguing and is explained, in the final analysis some would say, by **psychoanalytic theory**—a theory that many scholars in mass communication find untenable.

SUMMARY

In this chapter we have considered the focal points of interest in the study of mass communication: the artwork or text, the artist or creator, the audience, America or society, and the medium. We then examined how the terms *mass* and *communication* have been used by scholars with different points of view. This was followed by a discussion of Lasswell's formula; the models conceived by Gerbner, Osgood and Schramm, and Jakobson; Stephenson's play theory of mass communication; and the Sapir-Whorf hypothesis about the role language plays in shaping our conceptions of the world. We concluded with a discussion of controversies in the field and definition of some terms.

In the process of communication, a text is frequently interpreted against the background of codes different from those intended by the author. Some authors do not take into account such a possibility. They have in mind an average addressee referred to a given social context. Nobody can say what happens when the actual reader is different from the "average" one. Those texts that obsessively aim at arousing a precise response on the part of more or less precise empirical readers (be they children, soap-opera addicts, doctors, law-abiding citizens, swingers, Presbyterians, farmers, middle-class women, scuba divers, effete snobs, or any other imaginable sociopsychological category) are in fact open to any possible "aberrant" decoding. A text so immoderately "open" to every possible interpretation will be called a closed one. . . . This cannot happen with those I call "open" texts: they work at their peak revolutions per minute only when each interpretation is reechoed by the others, and vice versa. . . . You cannot use the text as you want, but only as the text wants you to use it. An open text, however "open" it be, cannot afford whatever interpretation.

Umberto Eco, *The Role of the Reader*, 1984

CHAPTER 2

THE ARTWORK (OR TEXT)

We have just examined mass communication in general and considered some of the more important models of the communication process. In this chapter, which focuses on the way texts can be interpreted, I deal with Akira Kurosawa's classic film *Rashomon*. I have chosen it because it is a masterpiece, but also because it serves as a metaphor for this book. In the film, as I will explain shortly, everyone who was involved with what happened in a grove offers a different description of what happened. What we have is what I call the "*Rashomon* phenomenon," which poses the question, Can we know reality and find the truth about it? To show how complicated texts are and how open they are to many kinds of analysis, I offer interpretations of the film that might be made by semioticians, psychoanalytic theorists, Marxists, feminists, sociologists, ethical theorists, myth/ritual/symbol critics, and aesthetic critics. I then discuss genres and formulas, as well as the essential formulaic aspects of some of the more common kinds of genre texts. I conclude with a discussion of an important social science methodology used to gain information about collections of texts, content analysis. This chapter prepares the way for Chapter 3, which addresses media, theories about media effects, and the question of violence.

AUTHOR'S NOTE: A variation of the section in this chapter on *Rashomon* was delivered in 1994 at the International Symposium on Film, Television and Video in Taipei, sponsored by Fu Jen Catholic University.

This chapter focuses on the films, television programs, and radio shows—what critics call texts—carried by the various media. The media, as noted in Chapter 1, play a role in shaping all texts, and I am mindful of that. This role of the media will be addressed in Chapter 3. I begin this chapter with discussion of a film that generally is thought to be one of the great masterpieces of the cinema, Akira Kurosawa's *Rashomon*.

Rashomon: A Synopsis

In this film, which takes place in the 12th century A.D., a priest, a woodcutter, and another man are in the Rashomon temple, seeking shelter from the rain. They frame the story, which concludes with a segment in which they find an abandoned baby, whom the woodcutter takes home with him to save from starving. The woodcutter narrates the tale, which takes the form of **flashbacks** from the points of view of each of the main characters in the story. It starts with Tajomaru, a famous bandit, who is dozing under a tree when he sees a samurai, Takehiro, passing with his wife, Masago, on a horse. She is heavily veiled, but a wisp of wind blows her veil aside and Tajomaru is astonished at her beauty and decides he must have her. Takehiro and his wife pass, but a short while later, Tajomaru accosts them. He tells Takehiro that there are some valuable swords nearby. Tajomaru leads Takehiro to a wooded spot, overpowers him, and ties him up. Then the bandit runs to Masago and tells her that Takehiro has been bitten by a snake. She follows him and finds her husband tied up. Masago tries to kill Tajomaru with a knife, but he subdues her. Tajomaru then has sex with Masago as Takehiro looks on. Afterward, Takehiro is killed. Unknown to the participants in this little melodrama, a woodcutter who is out searching for wood comes upon the

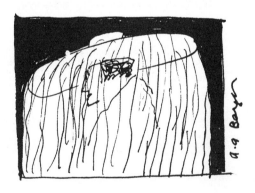

scene and, hidden in the forest, watches what transpires.

What follows is what gives this film its resonance. One by one, each participant and the woodcutter offer different accounts of what happened; their stories are depicted on-screen in a series of flashbacks as they testify in a prison courtyard. Each story justifies the behavior of the teller.

TAJOMARU'S VERSION OF WHAT HAPPENED

After having sex with Masago, who has given herself to him, Tajomaru is about to leave when she confronts him and says that he will have to fight her husband, and she will belong to whoever kills the other. As Tajomaru recounts the story, he has a long and difficult battle with Takehiro, who crosses swords with him 20 times before being killed. When Tajomaru then looks for Masago, he discovers that she has vanished.

MASAGO'S VERSION OF WHAT HAPPENED

According to Masago, Tajomaru runs off into the forest after he has raped her. She is sobbing hysterically and turns to look, broken-heartedly, at her husband. She sees cold hatred in his eyes. She finds her dagger and starts to cut the ropes that bind her husband. She pleads with him to stop looking at her with such hate-filled eyes. Takehiro says nothing and continues to stare at his wife. Eventually, in a hysterical fit, she plunges the dagger into his chest. She wanders to a pond and tries to drown herself, but is unable to do so.

TAKEHIRO'S VERSION OF WHAT HAPPENED

Because Takehiro is dead, a medium, a woman in a flowing gown, is called in to tell his version of what happened. She goes into a trance and makes connection with Takehiro in the world of the dead. The voice of Takehiro is heard, coming out of the mouth of the medium, telling his story. He says that after Tajomaru has had sex with Masago, he pleads with her to come with him. "Never," Takehiro says, "in all of our life together, had I seen her more beautiful." To his surprise, Masago agrees, but she insists that Tajomaru kill Takehiro. "As long as he is alive, I cannot go with you." This shocks the bandit, who suddenly feels revulsion for Masago. Tajomaru asks Takehiro what he wants done with Masago. She runs away and the bandit chases after her, leaving Takehiro alone. Tajomaru comes back hours later; it seems Masago has eluded him. He cuts Takehiro's bonds and leaves. The husband, tears rolling down his cheeks, takes a dagger and thrusts it into his own chest.

THE WOODCUTTER'S VERSION OF WHAT HAPPENED

We now come to the last version of what happened, the version told by the woodcutter. In this story, the bandit pleads with Masago to come with him and to become his wife. He promises to give up banditry. "Tell me you'll be my wife," he says. She says she cannot answer a question like that, and Tajomaru takes that to mean that the men must fight for her. Masago uses her dagger to cut the ropes that are restraining her husband, but when he is free, to Masago and Tajomaru's shock, Takehiro says that Tajomaru can take her. "I refuse to risk my life for such a woman." Masago looks at her husband with disbelief. The husband adds that he regrets the loss of his horse more than the loss of his wife. Eventually, Masago gets the two men to fight, and Tajomaru kills Takehiro, who is pleading for his life. What the woodcutter does not tell us, but we discover later, is that he has stolen Masago's dagger. The ghost of Takehiro mentions feeling the dagger being removed from his body, but we cannot be sure that Takehiro is telling the truth.

These four versions of what happened are the heart of the film, though there are other events in it that more or less frame it. The film is based on two short stories by Ryunosuke Akutagawa (1882-1927), "Rashomon" and "In a Grove." This synopsis says nothing of the brilliant camera work, editing, and acting in the film, but it does illustrate a very important point: It is very difficult to capture reality. Four people involved in a single episode in a grove can give four very different versions of what transpired.

The *Rashomon* Phenomenon

The *Rashomon* phenomenon raises this issue: How can we know reality and discern the truth? Is there a truth independent of the versions of each of the characters? Is one of the stories true, and are the others fabrications? If so, who is telling the truth, and how do we know? If you think about it, this phenomenon is at the heart of mystery stories, where there are many suspects, each of whom has an alibi, and it is the job of the detective to sort out all of the stories and find the truth. The same applies to legal cases, where various people who were at the scene of an accident or crime often tell different stories. But in *Rashomon* we never have a resolution.

I would like to suggest that the *Rashomon* story can be seen as a metaphor that has significance for our enterprise in this book, for it reflects the ways scholars and researchers with varying philosophical and methodological perspectives on mass communication deal with it, each coming up with something different. We learn that we must be skeptical about what people tell us.

In *Rashomon* we know nothing about the characters apart from the stories they tell, and we have to take their accounts of what happened in the grove at face value. The only thing they agree on is that Masago had sex with Tajomaru, but we cannot even be sure it was rape. According to Tajomaru's account, it was not. But can we trust his account? In the study of mass communication we must ask researchers to justify their methods and to show, to our satisfaction, how their theories explain events better than other theories do. And we must insist that the experiments they conduct can be replicated. But a great deal of the work done in mass communication is not based on experimentation; rather, researchers often try to explain data that others may have collected on phenomena of interest.

I have been talking about quantitative social science approaches here, which tend to focus on audiences and the media. When we look at texts such as *Rashomon,* we can employ many other methods, and it is to this subject, how one might interpret a text, that I would like to turn.

Analyzing and Interpreting Texts

Technically speaking, there is a difference between analysis and interpretation. *Analysis* generally is held to mean taking a text apart and considering how its various parts relate to one another. *Interpretation,* on the other hand, involves the use of some method or discipline—

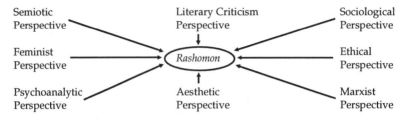

Figure 2.1. Disciplinary Perspectives on a Text

such as semiotic theory, psychoanalytic theory, or Marxist theory—
to figure out, to the extent that we can, how a text generates meaning
and affects people, and what it reflects about society and culture.

Let us take *Rashomon* as our example. I saw the film first in 1951 or
1952 at Smith College. I was a student majoring in English at the
University of Massachusetts, and I went with some of my friends and
some professors to see the film. In that audience, for argument's sake,
let us assume there were students with a number of different majors
and professors coming from a wide variety of disciplines. Each
person who saw *Rashomon* brought to the film his or her interests,
beliefs, background, fund of information, aesthetic sensibilities, and
so on, and each person, it is reasonable to suggest, saw his or her own
Rashomon, just as the characters in the film give different accounts of
what happened in that grove.

Figure 2.1 shows some of the more common ways of interpreting
a text; I will say something about each of them. There is no single
way to interpret a text, no "royal road" to understanding a text.
Rather, a large number of methods of analysis and techniques of
interpretation can be used to "read" texts, each of which has interesting and valuable insights to offer. Ultimately, I would argue, we use
as many techniques of interpretation as possible and try to fit them
together as best we can when dealing with texts.

Figure 2.1 depicts *Rashomon,* our text, in the center of an oval, with
the different techniques and methodologies that can be used to
interpret the film arrayed around it. Another text—for example, a
mystery story or television show or comic strip—could appear in the
center of such a chart, instead of *Rashomon*. My point is that just as

there are, so we are told, many ways to skin a cat, there are also many ways to interpret, analyze, "read" a text. Many of the techniques have affinities with others. For example, **semiotics** and psychoanalytic theory have many connections, and the same can be said for other methods or disciplines, such as psychoanalytic and feminist thought and sociological and Marxist thought.

We seldom think about it, but a great deal of what goes on in universities has to do with creativity and the works of creative artists, of one sort or another, in one medium or another. Departments such as literature, foreign languages, psychology, communication (or, in some institutions, communications), rhetoric, journalism, speech, art, history, anthropology, sociology, and political science often deal with texts and the media that carry and shape them. It should be noted that just as scholars in mass communication often disagree with one another, the same holds true of critics in literature departments, film departments, and all the other departments that deal with creative behavior and with artistic texts.

A Semiotic Interpretation of *Rashomon*

Semiotics is the science of signs, which are defined as anything that can be used to substitute or stand for something else. Semioticians are interested in how meaning is created in texts, and thus would be interested in the facial expressions of the characters, in the lighting and music used in the film, and in its narrative structure.

Vladimir Propp (1928/1968), one of the most famous theorists of narrativity whose work is used by semioticians, has elaborated a typology of different functions performed by characters in texts. This typology can be applied to *Rashomon* with interesting results. Table 2.1 presents an abbreviated application of Propp's functions to our text. We must remember Propp's analysis concerned several hundred Russian fairy tales, but his functions still can be applied, without too much difficulty, to *Rashomon* and many other narratives.

In addition, semioticians use the notion that meaning is connected to relationships and that texts generate their meaning, in part, by setting up a hidden structure of oppositions that helps us find out

TABLE 2.1 Proppian Analysis of *Rashomon*

Proppian Function		Application to Rashomon
α	initial situation	We see husband and wife.
β	absentation	Husband leaves wife to look at treasure.
η	trickery	Husband is lured to grove by bandit.
θ	complicity	Husband is overcome, "helps" bandit.
A	villainy	Bandit rapes wife in front of husband.
H	struggle	Husband and bandit battle.
L	unfounded claims	Each participant describes events in a self-serving way.
U	punishment	Each story involves punishment of one or more persons involved.

TABLE 2.2 Paradigmatic Analysis of *Rashomon*

Truth	Lies
what actually happened to	what supposedly happened to
bandit	bandit
wife	wife
husband	husband
woodcutter	woodcutter
reality	appearance
seeing what happens	selective perception
real reasons for actions	rationalizations for actions
faith in humankind	cynicism, skepticism

what the texts mean. This approach, called a *paradigmatic analysis,* is a modification of the work of the French structural anthropologist Claude Lévi-Strauss (1967). A paradigmatic analysis of *Rashomon* is presented in Table 2.2.

Semioticians suggest that texts are often related to other texts, a concept known as *intertextuality.* In the case of *Rashomon,* we know that an American film, *The Outrage,* was made in 1964 based on *Rashomon.* In addition, *Rashomon* can be related, intertextually, to other Japanese written and film texts involving samurai figures, and generically to all stories about heroic warriors and their battles. In this case, the samurai story is modified, and our samurai figure is outwitted, disgraced, and, according to some versions of the events, killed by the bandit.

A Psychoanalytic Interpretation of *Rashomon*

The film is a violent one and involves an attempt by Masago to kill Tajomaru with her dagger and her violent rape in front of her husband. We find, then, the matter of the power of sexuality and its link to violence elaborated. It is Tajomaru's desire for Masago that leads to the events that transpire. There is also an element of sadism, as Tajomaru rapes Takehiro's wife in front of him. Tajomaru says he wants to have Masago without killing her husband, if possible, but he does not have to rape her in front of her husband.

Using Freud's **id/ego/superego** typology, we would say that Tajomaru is an id-dominated person; he is a bandit who, we learn later, has killed many people. He has no impulse control and lacks a superego. None of the three main characters seems to have well-developed ego functions, though it is impossible to be sure about this because all of the stories conflict with one another. The one seemingly impartial observer, the woodcutter, has stolen Masago's dagger and lies about it, so we cannot be sure that even what he tells us is correct.

We also find **defense mechanisms** at work, in particular, **rationalization,** as each of the three main characters tells a story that is self-justifying, and denial, as the characters create wish-fulfilling fantasies to explain what happened. Masago claims that she was driven, by Takehiro's hatred and loathing, to kill him with her dagger. This might be seen as involving projection, in which one person's feelings are "projected" on to another. And Takehiro claims he was driven, by remorse and anguish over his wife's behavior, to kill himself.

A Marxist Interpretation of *Rashomon*

A Marxist critic would focus on the social and political factors that shape the behavior of the various characters. We have a confrontation between a lower-class villain, the bandit Tajomaru, who is constantly shown scratching himself and flicking flies away from himself, and an upper-class figure, Takehiro, a samurai, and his wife, Masago. It is Takehiro's desire for wealth, in the form of the swords Tajomaru tells him about, that leads him into Tajomaru's trap. And

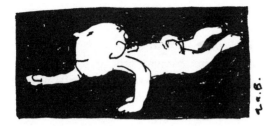

Takehiro's response to his wife's rape and her rejection of him is tied to his position as a samurai.

We also have the woodcutter, a representative of the working classes, who is forced to steal Masago's dagger to provide food for himself and his family. The woodcutter also rescues the abandoned baby. He has a large family; one more mouth to feed will not make much difference. He emerges as the only really heroic figure in the film. When the storm that has been pounding the Rashomon temple subsides, the woodcutter strides off with the abandoned baby in his arms, saving the child from starvation.

The fact that the baby has been abandoned is a strong indictment of the moral climate in the society in which the story takes place, but the blame is not put on the mother who abandoned the child because she could not feed it; rather, implicitly blamed are those who control the society and allow such conditions to exist.

A Feminist Interpretation of *Rashomon*

From the feminist perspective, what is of central importance is the fact that the film is about a rape. Tajomaru sees Masago and desires to have sex with her; if he can do so without killing her husband, he thinks, so much the better. She is, then, playing a typical role, that of sex object for a desiring male. Rape, of course, is not only a sexual matter, but also one involving dominance and submission. Thus when Masago tries to kill Tajomaru with her dagger, he becomes even more excited, for he will be able to dominate and rape a spirited woman. His interpretation of what happened, that she really surrendered to him, is highly suspect. We do not get this notion from any of the others involved in the story.

The portrayal of Masago by the various men is also interesting, because each gives a different picture of her. We see her in a number of different ways: as surrendering willingly to Tajomaru, which means she was not really raped; as a killer of her husband, driven to it by fit of temporary insanity caused by his hatred and loathing; as the breaker of her husband's heart, by suggesting that he must be killed by Tajomaru; and as a wily provocateur who is rejected by her husband (he says he does not want to fight for her, and regrets more the loss of his horse) but manages to tempt him and Tajomaru into fighting. She becomes a composite of many of the stereotypes men have about women, not only in the United States but in Japan, and presumably elsewhere as well.

The rape and the swordplay all point out, graphically, how **phallocentric** this text is; even the woman uses a dagger, a **phallic symbol,** though she drops it when subdued by Tajomaru, who does not resort to symbols but uses the real thing. *Rashomon* does not offer a sympathetic portrayal of Masago. In one version of the story she submits to her attacker, in another she kills her husband, in a third she breaks her husband's heart and drives him to suicide, and in a fourth she more or less tricks her husband and Tajomaru into fighting over her. She is even a failure at suicide.

The film reflects the tendency of many people, brainwashed women as well as men, to blame the victim of rape by suggesting that, either consciously or unconsciously, "she wanted it" and somehow communicated this, thus relieving men of responsibility for their actions.

A Sociological Interpretation of *Rashomon*

When sociologists look at individual texts, they concern themselves with the ways they can apply such concepts as **roles, status, gender, power, class, deviance, stereotypes, uses and gratifications,** and **values** to the specific text. (Sociologists vary and have different interests, of course; different ones would focus on different things.) They often combine concepts as well, and thus might talk about sex role stereotyping in a text or the values of the characters or the role of deviants. In this brief discussion I will focus on the aspect of **social class,** though I will use other concepts as well.

Rashomon is a story about a deviant—a bandit—and the impact his sexual lust has on his life and the lives of a samurai, the samurai's wife, and a woodcutter who happens, by chance, to observe the events that transpire. Tajomaru is portrayed as a kind of animal, always scratching himself and slapping flies, who forces himself (literally as well as figuratively) upon a husband and wife from a much more elevated social class. Tajomaru has a kind of animal energy and cunning that contrasts, vividly, with the serene and reserved nature of Masago. It is only by chance that a gust of wind sweeps her veils aside so that Tajomaru can see her. As a person without concern for mores and traditional values, and without any ability to defer his gratifications (which middle-class people are allegedly taught to do) or to concern himself very much with the consequences of his impulsive behavior, he decides to rape her.

As a sop to morality, Tajomaru decides to avoid killing the husband, if possible. In the film, we see that in two of the accounts he actually does kill the husband, whereas in the other accounts the husband is killed either by Masago or by himself. Suicide, a subject of considerable interest to sociologists, is individual behavior, but it is socially conditioned, affected by the values of the society and the groups to which one belongs.

Rashomon is, we must remember, a film full of violence that includes rape, a great deal of fighting and either murder or suicide, stealing, and an abandoned baby. We are so taken by the puzzle the story presents and by the aesthetic qualities of the film that we tend to lose sight of its violence and amorality. In the final scene, when the woodcutter, who has been exposed as a thief—he has stolen Masago's dagger to provide food for his family—takes the abandoned baby, the faith of the Rashomon temple priest is restored. This sentimental conclusion tends to make us forget how violent and amoral the main characters are.

An Ethical Interpretation of *Rashomon*

Moralistic or **ethical criticism** has a long history. The focus in this approach is on the moral aspects of the beliefs and actions of the characters in a text. The main ethical problem that *Rashomon* raises is the matter of **relativism,** for each of the characters involved tells a different, self-justifying story of what happened in the grove, after the rape—or, as Tajomaru tells it, after what he depict as a violent seduction. But rapists cannot be expected to incriminate themselves, generally speaking, so we have to take his "evidence" with a grain of salt.

If we generalize from the film to real life, we find ourselves with a dilemma. In a world in which different peoples have varying practices and beliefs, some of which may be abhorrent to us, can we say that our values and beliefs are the correct ones and all others are wrong? This position, known as **ethnocentrism,** is not morally defensible. We face a problem: Are there objective standards that apply to all people everywhere? And if we believe that there are such standards, moral absolutes, certain values and beliefs that should be universal, how do we decide which ones should be the absolutes?

Most of us, no doubt, react viscerally to the violence in the story, and are repelled by it. We probably also are disturbed by the way each of the characters involved tells a story that justifies his or her actions. But from all of this comes a sense of skepticism and cynicism, a feeling that we cannot know the truth and cannot trust what people tell us—two positions that lead to an amoral perspective on life.

The film raises another moral problem. The woodcutter steals Masago's jeweled dagger and lies about doing so, in order to have money to feed his family. Is he right in doing so? The problem is more or less hedged by the ending, in which he takes the abandoned baby, but there is still a moral dilemma raised by his actions: Is it right to do wrong for good purposes? Do the ends justify the means, or are they so strongly connected that using immoral means taints moral ends? These are the kinds of questions ethical critics raise. It is obvious that there are no easy solutions to such questions, for it is the value system of the ethical critics that shapes their criticism, and different ethical critics have different, and often opposing, values.

A Myth/Ritual/Symbol Interpretation of *Rashomon*

Some critics focus on the mythic, ritualistic, and symbolic dimensions of texts. It is obvious that in doing so they share interests with semiotic and psychoanalytic critics, but critical perspectives often overlap one another, and some critics, as I have pointed out, are multidisciplinary in their approaches. Let me, in this brief section, suggest a couple of topics that would fall under this kind of analysis.

Tajomaru can be described in many respects as a **trickster figure.** As Joseph Henderson (1968) notes, a "trickster is a figure whose physical appetites dominate his behavior; he has the mentality of an infant. Lacking any purpose beyond the gratification of his primary needs, he is cruel, cynical and unfeeling" (pp. 102-103). According to this definition, there seems to be good reason to suggest that there is a strong trickster element in Tajomaru's personality.

James F. Davidson (1969) has suggested that Tajomaru can be related to Japanese folklore:

> He appears the least Japanese of all the characters, and a sort of incarnation of the *oni* or ogre of Japanese folklore, which has often been interpreted as a representation of the foreigner. His build and movements, even his features, suggest something of the gangling awkwardness that appears in Japanese caricatures of Occidentals. He is alternately terrifying and ridiculous, but always alien to the others. (p. 215)

There are reasons to suggest, then, that Tajomaru has what might be called "mythic" dimensions, and that the story has broader meaning than might seem to be the case.

What gives *Rashomon* its resonance is the fact that its characters have symbolic meaning; it is not simply a story about four individuals, but ultimately is about human beings in general and the problems our passions and pretenses pose for us. The characters are what Jungians would call **archetypes,** and their actions call forth in audiences reactions that are tied, Jungians believe, to unconscious content in the human mind passed down over the generations. Tajomaru would represent the **shadow** elements in our personalities, the evil elements that we keep repressed—but that nevertheless we intuitively recognize—and that play a role in the emotional responses we feel when we see the film (or any work of art, by extension).

An Aesthetic Interpretation of *Rashomon*

I have always felt that much mass communication research neglects textual analysis, seeing it instead as a kind of literary or humanistic enterprise and not as yielding quantitative data that can be massaged using various statistical techniques. But in neglecting textual criticism in general, and aesthetic interpretations of texts in particular, mass communication scholars have only impoverished themselves and weakened their arguments.

Aesthetic analysis involves the interpretation of aesthetic elements in a text, such as the use of lighting, sound effects, music, shot selection, cutting, editing, and flashbacks on the technical side, and the power of the work of actors and actresses on the performance side. For example, a simple count of the number of images of violence in a text can be misleading if there is one image of violence that is of central importance.

Rashomon has a number of celebrated scenes, such as one in which the woodcutter is running through the forest with the sunlight streaming through the trees and reflecting off his ax; another famous scene depicts the "long kiss" with which Tajomaru overpowers Masago, who surrenders willingly (so he claims) to her lustful desires. The camera work in this film is remarkable, as is the use of sound and music and the highly stylized nature of the acting. Aesthetic critics might also consider the use of flashbacks and the segmented structure of the film.

In addition to the methods of interpretation I have sketched out above, there are many others that could be used. One could take a traditional "literary critical" approach, which deals with plot, theme, tone, and related concerns. Or one could address the political aspects of the text and the relationships of dominance and submission found in the text. The point I want to make is that mass communication researchers neglect textual interpretation at their peril, for the texts that are carried and shaped by the media that carry them are extremely complex and require analysis as texts.

A Theoretical Matter: The Functions of Texts

In his classic work of literary criticism, *The Mirror and the Lamp*, M. H. Abrams (1958) discusses a number of theories about the nature and functions of the arts. There are, he suggests, four basic kinds of theories about the nature and roles of texts and works of art in the most general understanding of the term: **mimetic** theories, **objective** theories,

> The essential nature of art will be found neither in the production of objects to satisfy practical needs, nor in the expression of religious or philosophic ideas, but in its capacity to create a synthetic and self-conscious world . . . a mode, therefore, of envisaging the individual's perception of some aspect of universal truth. In all its essential activities, art is trying to tell us something about the universe, something about nature, about man, or about the artist, himself.
>
> Herbert Read, *Art and Society*, 1966, p. 2

expressive theories, and **pragmatic** theories. I briefly explain these theories below, drawing upon Abrams's ideas. I recommend his book for those interested in pursuing these matters in more detail.

Mimetic theories. Mimetic theories focus on the way art imitates life, and thus see art as a mirror. Some mimetic critics argue that the arts imitate the world of appearance and not the world of essence (the real world) and thus have a secondary status in the scheme of things, relative to truth itself.

Objective theories. Abrams's lamp is the symbolic manifestation of objective theories. Art projects its own reality, and the function of critics is, in essence, to examine the internal relations of the elements in a work of art. As Abrams puts it, "The 'objective orientation' which on principle regards the work of art in isolation . . . analyzes it as a self-sufficient entity constituted by its part in their internal relations, and sets out to judge it solely by criteria intrinsic to its own mode of being" (p. 26).

Pragmatic theories. Pragmatism focuses on the consequences of our actions. Thus pragmatic theories of art concern themselves with the effects of works of art on their audiences—the way these works inform people, persuade people, motivate people, and move people.

TABLE 2.3 Theories of Art and Artworks

Theory of Art	Work of Art's Mode of Operation	Focus
Mimetic	(mirror) imitates reality	society
Objective	(lamp) projects reality	work of art
Pragmatic	functions for people	audience
Expressive	emotional reactions	artist

Expressive theories. Expressive theorists stress the imaginative and inventive aspects of texts, seeing them as expressions of the psyches of artists, writers, filmmakers, and others involved in various aspects of textual creation.

These four types of theories are allied to a schema that Abrams elaborates involving what he calls "the co-ordinates of art criticism": a work, its audiences, the artists who create it, and the universe or nature. His book is devoted, for the most part, to the criticism of romantic literature. For purposes of this discussion, I have considerably modified Abrams's coordinates, because my concerns are different. I have added media to his list and substituted America (society) for what he calls the universe in developing my focal points because I am interested in studying mass communication. Table 2.3 displays the four kinds of theories of art.

If we apply these different theories to *Rashomon* (depending upon which we think are most tenable and best describe things), we can see the film as one of the following:

1. an imitation of what people are really like
2. a text whose elements are so beautifully integrated that it has a powerful impact on people
3. a work that teaches us about the complexity of human relationships and the power of sexuality (so that we can be on our guard)
4. an expression of Kurosawa's insights and artistic powers

But the theories are all very abstract, and we would still need to make the kinds of analysis suggested above, using different disciplines to interpret the text. Naturally, the techniques we use would be affected by our views about the nature of artistic works.

Defining Texts

I have already offered a basic definition of what a text is. Texts are, in the simplest sense, works that are carried on media. In some cases, however, things become complicated. For example, what is the text in a soap opera that has been running for 20 years? Is it the series itself, or can we isolate some aspects of the series or some key episodes and use them as our text?

How do we deal with **serial texts** such as soap operas or situation comedies that have been broadcast continually over extended periods? Or comic strips that have been published for 40 or 50 years? I would suggest that it is impossible to deal with such texts except by taking some shortcuts: We can describe the series in very general terms and then focus our attention on what we consider to be significant episodes. The series becomes the ground and provides context, whereas the key episodes become the figure, on which we focus our attention.

The distinguished Russian semiotician and literary theorist Yuri (Jurij) Lotman offers a number of valuable insights about texts in his book *The Structure of the Artistic Text* (1977). A few of these may be expressed, in summarized and somewhat simplified form, as follows:

1. Language is our primary coding or modeling system, and works of art are special means of communication that involve a **secondary modeling system.** Thus words are part of language and our primary modeling system. When we use these words to write a novel, creating a work with a certain structure, we move up a level to a secondary modeling system.
2. Everything in an artistic text is meaningful, and nothing should be considered accidental.
3. Artistic texts are so complex that they transmit different messages to different readers, viewers, or audience members, based on their level of comprehension.

As Lotman puts it, the artistic text

transmits different information to different readers in proportion to each one's comprehension; it provides the reader with a language in which each successive portion of information may be assimilated with repeated reading. It behaves as a kind of living organism which has a feedback channel to the reader and thereby instructs him. (p. 23)

That explains why we can read novels over and over again and get different things out of them, and why we can do the same with films, television programs, and other texts.

Lotman uses the phrase "multiply encoded" to refer to the complexity of texts, the reasons they are so rich and can be interpreted in so many different ways, and the problems we have in making sense of them. Those interested in this aspect of mass communication research would be well advised to read Lotman's book. There are a number of other works, as well, that deal with the nature of texts and intertextuality, the relation of texts to one another.

Understanding Genres

When we watch television, we are always watching a text that can be classified as a **genre** or particular kind of program. Let's take a family: One person likes soap operas, another likes sports programs, a third likes situation comedies, a fourth likes news programs, and a fifth likes religious programs. Viewers often watch television because they like certain genres rather than particular shows (I discuss this matter in some detail in Chapter 4). Genres rise and fall in popularity. At one time, for example, there were close to 40 western series on television; then we lost interest in them, and now there are hardly any westerns, although in recent years they seem to be making a comeback of sorts.

Genres are formulaic in nature. That is, within a given genre, there are certain kinds of characters, plots, locations, situations, heroes, villains, and so on. We quickly learn the conventions of a genre and expect to find them, though they can be modified considerably, when we watch a certain genre television program or read a certain genre book: classical detective, tough-guy detective, spy story, science fiction, horror story, western, or romance, for example. Sometimes genres are combined, as in the western/romance story, or in science fiction/horror.

John Cawelti (1971) discusses the nature of **formulas:**

Most of the criteria by which we might judge a classically constructed narrative fall by the wayside when we look at these games as storytelling systems. In Nintendo's narratives, characters play a minimal role, displaying traits that are largely capacities for action: fighting skills, modes of transportation, preestablished goals. The games' dependence on characters (Ninja Turtles, Bart Simpson, etc.) borrowed from other media allows them to simply evoke these characters rather than to fully develop them. The character is little more than a cursor that mediates the players' relationship to the story world. Activity drains away the characters' strength, as measured by an ever shifting graph at the top of the screen, but it cannot build character, since these figures lack even the most minimal interiority. Similarly, plot is transformed into a generic atmosphere—a haunted house, a subterranean cavern, a futuristic city-scape, an icy wilderness—that the player can explore.

> Mary Fuller and Henry Jenkins, "Nintendo and New World
> Travel Writing," 1995, p. 61

All cultural products contain a mixture of two elements: conventions and inventions. Conventions are elements which are known to both the creator and his audience beforehand—they consists of things like favorite plots, stereotyped characters, accepted ideas, commonly known metaphors and other linguistic devices, etc. Inventions, on the other hand, are elements which are uniquely imagined by the creator such as new kinds of characters, ideas, or linguistic forms. (p. 27)

Romance novels are extremely conventional and formulaic, whereas certain other kinds of works—such as James Joyce's *Ulysses* or *Finnegan's Wake*, which make their readers do a great deal of work and are not easy to understand (some might say impossible to understand)—are very inventive.

TABLE 2.4 Formulaic Elements in Selected Genres

	Genre		
Element	*Western*	*Science Fiction*	*Spy*
Location	edge of civilization	space	world
Time	1800s	future	present
Hero	cowboy	spaceman	agent
Heroine	schoolmarm	spacegal	woman spy
Secondary characters	townsfolk, Indians	technicians	other spies
Villains	outlaws	aliens	moles
Plot	restore law	repel aliens	find moles
Themes	justice	save humanity	save free world
Costume	cowboy hat	high-tech, sleek clothes	suit
Locomotion	horses	spaceships	planes
Weaponry	six-gun	ray gun	pistol with silencer

SOURCE: Adapted from Berger (1992).

Table 2.4 lists some of the basic components of some of our most popular genres and the formulaic ways in which these stories are constructed. It is probably because they are working with formulas that television writers can write scripts quickly enough to meet the scheduling demands of the medium. These writers can count on their audiences knowing a great deal and can adapt and modify basic plots, putting in enough invention so that audiences won't be bored, but keeping enough formulaic elements so they won't be confused.

Genre theory has been somewhat neglected for a long time, but in recent years researchers have become interested in the nature of genres and the role they play in mass communication. Genres mediate between particular texts on one side, and between the media and mass communication in general on the other. They help us understand how texts are created, how texts relate to one another, and why people might like them.

The most significant genre on radio and television, I would argue, is the commercial, just as the most significant genre in print media is the advertisement. Those who own the mass media use their texts and genres, it has been suggested, primarily to sell audiences to advertisers. It is not too much of an exaggeration to argue that programs and news stories, and other similar genres, have been reduced to the status of filler between commercials and advertisements. Texts have to attract the right audiences for the products being advertised, and a great deal of attention is devoted to finding the right text and genre for a given product.

Television commercials cost many times more per minute than the programs that carry them. It costs a million dollars, more or less, to make an hour-long action-adventure program, but it can cost $350,000 for a 30-second commercial. In some cases the commercials have more entertainment value than the programs in which they are found, but this is understandable, given that they can cost 10 times as much, on a per minute basis, as the programs that carry them.

Content Analysis

Let me conclude this chapter on textual analysis with a discussion of **content analysis,** a methodology used by social scientists that does not examine particular texts but looks at collections of texts to see what they reveal about our beliefs and values. According to George V. Zito (1975):

> Content analysis may be defined as a methodology by which the researcher seeks to determine the manifest content of written, spoken, or published communication by *systematic, objective,* and *quantitative* analysis. . . . Since any written communication (and this includes novels, plays, and television scripts as well as personal letters, suicide notes, magazines, and newspaper accounts), is produced by a communicator, the *intention of the communicator* may be the object of our research. Or we may be interested in the audience, or *receiver* of the communication, and may attempt to determine something about it. (p. 27)

When we make a content analysis, we try to learn something about people who create texts by making a quantitative study of some topic as it is found in some collection of their texts. We also can make inferences about what readers or viewers of the texts being analyzed might be getting out of them, but that is very risky. As Chaim Eyal (personal communication, 1994) explains:

Most social scientists who carry out content analyses would probably disagree with the last two paragraphs of the Zito quotation [above]. Through content analyses researchers could test hypotheses about sources, messages, and channels, but *not about audiences* (or the readers of texts). In fact, the quote . . . from Zito contains a glaring contradiction: If content analysis is the study of *manifest content* (as was originally articulated by Bernard Berelson), then how could the analyst possibly draw conclusions about the reader—actual or intended? To do so requires making assumptions and jumping to conclusions that cannot possibly be supported by the text. This would clearly render the analysis *nonobjective*—another violation of the method.

Eyal points out a problem faced by people making content analyses— they find it hard to refrain from making inferences about the audiences of the texts and what these audiences are getting out of the text.

There is a reason for this. It is generally assumed that people want to avoid **cognitive dissonance**—that is, they want to avoid exposing themselves to ideas that run counter to their basic beliefs and values. It is also assumed that one of the main functions of the mass media is to reinforce people in their convictions. Thus people would avoid material not congruent with their beliefs and would seek out material that reinforces their beliefs; if this were always true, researchers would have good reason for making inferences about audiences and texts. But the fact remains that inferences about audiences are not objective and are not based on empirical evidence.

Another perspective is offered by Jeremy Butler (1994), who describes the methodology of content analysis (in this case, of television texts) as follows:

A textual component is selected based on the researcher's theoretical interests: e.g., sexual behavior in prime-time programs, or sickness and death in soap operas. The researcher observes the television text and counts the number of occurrences of this component in a program's manifest content, the characters and their actions. (Content analysis seldom addresses television's stylistic aspects.) These data are then "coded" (converted through categorization) into statistical form. From studies such as these we can learn that incidents of hugging in prime-time TV occurred at a rate of .80 per hour during the week of February 2-8, 1989, or that 5.3 percent of soap opera characters die in car accidents. (p. 293)

One of the problems with content analysis concerns the interpretation of the data it yields. As Butler points out, viewers interpret what they see on television one way and what happens in real life another way, so the data we get from content analysis may not be very useful: "Television and other art forms transmogrify life. The aesthetic text recontextualizes elements from real life in ways that give them new meanings" (p. 293). That is why, I would suggest, we must consider other ways of dealing with texts, as elaborated in the discussion of *Rashomon,* as complementary to content analysis. Data cannot tell us everything.

In the early 1940s, Leo Lowenthal, a prominent sociologist, made a celebrated content analysis of biographical magazine articles in popular American weeklies. He contrasted what he found in a study of a year's worth of *Collier's* and the *Saturday Evening Post* and what his research into biographies written in earlier years showed. He discovered that the early biographies tended to focus on "idols of production," people such as bankers and industrialists and inventors who contributed to the growth of the economy in a society where opportunity was seen as open to everyone and who functioned as models for people. Later biographies showed a change; they were about "idols of consumption"—celebrities, actresses and actors, sports heroes, and entertainers—and focused on their **lifestyles** and their leisure—how they lived, what they owned, what they purchased (Lowenthal, 1944).

Lowenthal suggests that his content analysis reveals a major transformation that had taken place in American society. He offers a number of quotations from the articles he examined to support his contentions, and analyzes the language found in many articles that made great use of superlatives. The later biographies did not function, as earlier ones had, as a source of orientation for their readers; instead, they led to a dream world for the masses, where they no longer concerned themselves with social and political matters but focused their attention on consumption. Lowenthal's article, which is more than 40 pages long, concludes as follows:

> It is some comfort for the little man who has become expelled from the Horatio Alger dream, who despairs of penetrating the thicket of grand strategy in politics and business, to see his heroes as a lot of guys who

like or dislike highballs, cigarettes, tomato juice, golf and social gatherings—just like himself. He knows how to converse in the sphere of consumption and here he can make no mistakes. By narrowing his focus of attention, he can experience the gratification of being confirmed in his own pleasures and discomforts by participating in the pleasures and discomforts of the great. The large confusing issues in the political and economic realm and the antagonisms in the social realm—all these are submerged in the experience of being at one with the lofty and great in the sphere of consumption. (pp. 547-548)

Lowenthal's words, written so many years ago, still have a ring of truth. On the other hand, there are reasons to question Lowenthal's methodology and his selection of quotations, for example.

SUMMARY

This chapter began with a synopsis of the classic film *Rashomon* and then used a variety of techniques and disciplinary approaches to interpret it. Next, M. H. Abrams's (1958) four theories about the nature of art—mimetic, objective, pragmatic, and expressive—were introduced. This was followed by a discussion of the nature of texts and by a section on genre theory. The chapter concluded with an explanation of content analysis and of a celebrated example of this methodology, Leo Lowenthal's "Biographies in Popular Magazines," which was published in 1944.

Ask someone raised in the religious traditions of the Western world to describe God, and this, with idiosyncratic variations, might be the answer:

"God is all-knowing, and all-powerful. He is a spirit, not a body, and He exists both outside us and within us. God is always with us, because He is everywhere. We can never fully understand Him, because He works in mysterious ways."

In broad terms, this describes the God of our fathers, but it also describes the electronic media, the second god, which man has created.

Tony Schwartz, *Media: The Second God*, 1983

CHAPTER 3

MEDIA

Having examined the complexities involved in interpreting a text, we move on to a discussion of media. I begin with an examination of some of the more interesting theories about media and the way the media function, such as transportation theory, responsive chord theory, and Marshall McLuhan's theories about hot and cool media. Next, I address various theories about media effects, such as those regarding the agenda-setting and gatekeeping functions of media, cultivation theory, reinforcement theory, spiral of silence theory, and the question of cultural imperialism. This is followed by a discussion of what research suggests about media effects (are they powerful or weak), the ownership of the media (if the media have few effects, it matters little who owns them), and the problem of violence and the media (if the media have weak effects, the fact that they are full of violence is of little importance). If the media have powerful effects, which is probably the dominant position in media studies, their ownership and the issue of the violence they contain become very important. I point out that there are a number of different kinds of violence in the media, and that there are many ways of thinking about it. I conclude with a consideration of the generally neglected matter of media aesthetics. This chapter is preparation for the material in Chapter 4, on the audiences that media try to reach with their texts.

A **medium**, as we generally understand the term in the study of mass communication, is a means of transmitting some kind of text. For example, we have electronic media, such as radio and television, that carry certain kinds (or genres) of programs, such as commercials, news shows, soap operas, talk shows, music programs, situation comedies, action-adventure shows, science fiction shows, and sporting events. And we have print media, such as books, magazines, newspapers, and billboards, that carry texts as varied as novels, plays, news articles, publicity releases, advertisements, and comic strips. Playing increasingly important roles in our everyday lives now also are video games and the mixed and interactive media of CD-ROM.

We should always be mindful of the distinctions among a medium, the genres it carries, and the specific texts we watch, listen to, look at, read, and so on. Generally speaking, we tend to blur the distinctions; we talk about watching television, listening to radio, and seeing films. This kind of language is correct as far as it goes, but it is not very precise. When we watch television, we are always watching some specific program (which is representative of a particular genre), and when we listen to the radio we always are listening to a particular program that broadcasts news, music, talk, or whatever. In addition, when we watch television we also listen to television, though we seldom seem to pay much attention to this aspect of our involvement with the television medium.

It is useful to remember that media carry texts and that each medium shapes, in various ways, the texts it carries. Also, we should keep in mind, as I have already pointed out, that when we talk about the media (unless we are specifically considering media aesthetics), generally we are talking about the texts the media carry and not the media themselves, as divorced from their texts. In this chapter I will separate the mass media from their texts to the extent possible, but we must keep in mind that texts, media, audiences, and artists are all intimately connected.

Transportation, Responsive Chord, and Ritual Theories of Media

When I use the term *carry* in regard to what media do with texts, I am offering the most commonly understood sense of what a medium is—something that transports, or carries, texts and delivers them to audiences. In Roman Jakobson's model of the communication process (discussed in Chapter 1), a sender encodes a message and sends it via some medium to a receiver who decodes the message. For example, in a conversation, a speaker has ideas or messages he or she wishes to send to the receiver; the speaker puts these messages into the form of spoken words, which are then decoded and made sense of by the receiver. When the receiver decodes the message more or less as the sender sent it, and gets the meaning that the sender wanted to send, we say that there has been effective communication—that is, a transfer of information without significant distortion.

Tony Schwartz (1974) describes this transfer of meaning or information as an example of the "transportation" theory of communication. But there is another way of thinking about communication that he believes is also important—what he calls "responsive chord" theory. He explains this understanding of communication, especially as it relates to electronic media and advertising, as follows:

> Many of our experiences with electronic media are coded and stored in the same way they are perceived. Since they do not undergo a symbolic transformation, the original experience is more directly available to us when it is recalled. Also, since the experience is not stored in a symbolic form, it cannot be retrieved by symbolic cues. It must be evoked by a stimulus that is coded the same way as the stored information is coded.
>
> The critical task is to design our package of stimuli so that it resonates with information already stored within an individual and thereby induces the desired learning or behavioral effect. Resonance takes place when the stimuli put into our communication evoke *meaning* in a listener or viewer. (pp. 24-25)

What this suggests is that the function of the communicator, in many cases, is not to transfer new information but to strike a responsive chord, utilizing the information already stored in the mind of the listener or viewer.

We make use, to varying degrees, of some of the information that the people we are communicating with already know, which means that we use media, in a sense, to press people's buttons, and not to transfer data or information, especially when it comes to making commercials and trying to persuade people to buy some product or service. Using notions people already have in their minds (that Rolls Royce is a sign of wealth, for instance) is an example of what semioticians call **metonymy**, a rhetorical device that generates meaning by using associations.

As a result of watching television almost 4 hours a day (or 28 hours a week), the typical American is exposed to a great deal of information on all kinds of subjects in the form of **images** and speech. In addition to this mediated information we can add what people learn as they go through the educational process, in their social relations, and from other media, such as newspapers, magazines, and books. The task of the advertiser, as Schwartz explains it, is not to sell products or services to people only by giving them new information, but to sell products and services also by using the information they already have.

There is another way to look at our media usage, and that is as a functional alternative to religion. This view emphasizes the ritualistic, repetitive element of media use and the media dependencies that some people develop. Many people watch certain programs regularly and can even be said to be "devoted" (a term with religious connotations) to these programs. We even say that people who never miss certain soap operas or game shows watch those shows *religiously*. To the extent that our viewing television or listening to certain radio programs or reading certain publications is highly regular and psychologically important to us, it can be said that there is a ritualistic dimension to our media usage.

Media use is generally connected to specific texts or to particular genres carried by certain media (such as romance novels); the relationship between the medium and the text is a complicated one that needs to be considered. Schwartz's theory of media as hitting responsive chords in people still separates media from the content (texts) carried by the media. The late Marshall McLuhan, however, made no such separation. It is to his theories, now somewhat neglected (or perhaps discredited), that we turn next.

McLuhan's Theory: The Medium Is the Message

In the first chapter of his book *Understanding Media* (1965), McLuhan argues that "the medium is the message." According to McLuhan,

TABLE 3.1 McLuhan on the Differences Between Print and Electronic Media

Print Media	Electronic Media
eye/visual	aural
linear	all at once
logic	emotion
connected	simultaneous
rationality, logic	the mythic
the book	the radio
individualism	community
detachment	involvement
separation	connection
data classification	pattern recognition

what is most important are the media people watch or listen to, not the programs or texts carried by the media. As he explains: "The effects of technology do not occur at the level of opinions or concepts, but alter sense ratios or patterns of perception steadily and without any resistance" (p. 18). McLuhan asserts that the media profoundly affect the way we make sense of the world, so they are much more important, his theory implies, than the texts they carry.

He offers the example of print and what might be described as the hidden but logical imperatives that come from the impact of print on our psyches and society: the importance of the eye and seeing, linearity, standardization, rationality, continuity, individualism, nationalism, specialization, the assembly line (in factories), and railroads. He contrasts print with electronic media, which are aural, involve all-at-onceness, and simultaneity (instead of separation and linear development). These differences are sketched out in Table 3.1, which deals with oppositions I have elicited from McLuhan's writings. The table suggests that print media and electronic media lead to different sensibilities and perspectives on things. Print media lead to an approach that involves classifying data, whereas electronic media teach us to look for patterns. Think, for example, of the difference between looking at statistics and listening to music.

It is not the content of print and electronic media so much as the media themselves that are important for McLuhan. In dismissing the content of the media as of secondary importance, McLuhan, it can be argued, neglects an important aspect of the media—programs or

texts—and places too much stress on the media per se. Nevertheless, his theory does call attention to a matter we tend to neglect when we focus on the texts carried by the media, namely, the role the media play in the scheme of things and the way the media may be profoundly shaping our senses.

McLuhan had another theory, discussed in the second chapter of *Understanding Media*, that also generated a great deal of controversy. It is to that topic I now turn—his classification of some media as "hot" and other media as "cool."

McLuhan's Theory of Hot and Cool Media

McLuhan (1965) explains the differences between hot and cool media as follows:

> There is a basic principle that distinguishes a hot medium like radio from a cool one like the telephone, or a hot medium like the movie from a cool one like TV. A hot medium is one that extends one single sense in "high definition." High definition is the state of being well filled with data. A photograph is visually "high definition." A cartoon is "low definition," simply because very little visual information is provided. Telephone is a cool medium, or one of low definition, because the ear is given a meager amount of information. And speech is a cool medium of low definition, because so little is given and so much has to be filled

TABLE 3.2 McLuhan on Hot and Cool Media

Hot	*Cool*
high definition	low definition
much information	little information
low participation	high participation
excludes	includes
radio	telephone
movie	television
photograph	cartoon
printed word	speech
phonetic alphabet	hieroglyphics
lecture	seminar
advanced countries	backward countries
city slicker	rustic
waltz	twist
nylon stockings	open mesh stockings
F.D.R.	Coolidge
symphony broadcast	symphony rehearsal

in by the listener. On the other hand, hot media do not leave so much to be filled in or completed by the audience. Hot media are, therefore, low in participation, and cool media are high in participation or completion by the audience. Naturally, therefore, a hot medium like radio has very different effects on the user from a cool medium like the telephone. (pp. 22-23)

According to McLuhan's definitions, then, it is possible to classify various media as hot or cool, depending upon how much information they give. This classification is useful because it offers us insight into the way media function and the effects the different media might have on individuals and societies. Table 3.2 lists hot and cool media in terms of polar opposites, as McLuhan has done. All of these oppositions are elicited from his chapter on hot and cool media and are rather obvious, once you see them. A lecture, for example, is hot, because the audience can listen only to the speaker, whereas a seminar is cool because all attendees can participate in conveying the information.

McLuhan's notion about hot and cool media is meant to explain why certain media are so powerful, but there are problems with this division. According to McLuhan, film is a hot medium. When we watch a film, we see images flashed upon a screen in rapid succession.

There is a great deal of information, in contrast to the television screen, which is made up of dots that we have to turn into images. But films are often extremely engrossing, which, in principle, they should not be—relative to television, that is. McLuhan argues that film and television are different in that we look at a projected image when we watch a film, but when we watch television, we become the screen, so to speak, and the images are projected onto us. With television we have to work hard to make sense of the dots we find on the screen, and therefore television should be much more powerful than film. But it seems that when people watch television, they are often not engrossed in it at all; they may do homework, carry on conversations, or take part in other activities at the same time.

McLuhan created a big sensation for a few years or so in the 1960s. Then interest in his ideas faded and he was not so much rejected as forgotten about, as other theories came to the attention of those interested in mass communication. One reason he has been neglected in recent years is that although his ideas are interesting and provocative, they have not generated any important theories. Also his style, which smacked of advertising (the advertising agencies were very interested in his work) and sloganeering, put off a number of scholars, who found his insouciance and smart-alecky style distasteful. He was also attacked as being a popularizer and as having taken most of his ideas from others.

Ironically, McLuhan rejected what certainly is one of his most important books, *The Mechanical Bride* (1951), because it focuses on content, on texts carried by various media, and not on media per se. This book, which deals with advertising, comics, and various artifacts and objects and what they reflect about our values and beliefs, is a major contribution to our understanding of popular culture and everyday life.

Media Effects

THE SOCIOPOLITICAL IMPACT OF MEDIATED NARRATIVES

We seldom think about it, but a significant percentage of the texts carried on television (the dominant medium in terms of the time we spend watching it) are narratives, stories about people who have adventures, who do things. This point is made by Martin Esslin in his book *The Age of Television* (1982):

> On the most obvious level television is a dramatic medium simply because a large proportion of the material it transmits is in the form of traditional drama, consisting of fictional material mimetically represented by actors and employing plot, dialogue, character, gesture, costume—the whole panoply of dramatic means of expression. . . . The time devoted by the average American adult male to watching dramatic material on television thus amounts to over 12 hours per week, while the average American woman sees almost 16 hours of drama on television each week. That means that the average American adult sees the equivalent of *five to six full-length stage plays a week!* (p. 7)

Esslin's figures are based on statistics gathered in 1976-1977; since then, television viewing has increased, and there is good reason to believe that our exposure to televised narratives also has increased. Esslin adds that there are dramatic components to genres that are not seen as dramatic, such as game shows, sports programs (which are elaborately staged), and commercials, which can be seen as micro-dramas. Even news programs can be seen as forming narratives, though the narrativity of the news is imposed, unconsciously, by the viewer.

Dramas on television communicate to a great degree through images. They make use of various technical devices, such as costumes, props, lighting, music, certain kinds of camera shots, and editing, to generate emotions in people. As Esslin (1982) puts it, "In drama the complex, multilayered image predominates over the spoken word" (p. 22). We learn to see the world as it is filtered through personalities, and this tends to downplay such other elements as our thinking and reasoning about social and political issues. A good example of this comes from a study that used a particular broadcast network television news story about Ronald Reagan to test what people recall from such stories. In the news story used in the study, the newscaster said very negative things about Reagan, who was also shown in video clips in various settings. When viewers were later questioned about the story, they reported remembering best the images of Reagan, and their impressions of the story were that it was

TABLE 3.3 Media Effects Theories

socialization theory
agenda-setting theory
gatekeeping theory
cultivation theory
reinforcement theory
spiral of silence theory
cultural imperialism theory

positive; they had paid relatively little attention to what was said by the reporter.

Television, Esslin adds, brings an endless stream of collective daydreams and fantasies into our homes, and this leads to a blurring of the difference between fact and reality, the real world and the fantasy world. Thus the medium of television, because it is so well suited to carrying dramatic genres, has important social and political consequences (see Table 3.3).

SOCIALIZATION

The media now play an increasingly important role in our **socialization**—the process by which we learn how to become members of society. We are socialized to take on various roles, or patterns of behavior and conduct, and certain values, attitudes, and beliefs, which are all tied in various ways to socioeconomic class, race, religion, ethnicity, and other aspects of our social identity—especially, now, our media usage. Before the development of mass media, an individual's socialization was more or less tied to his or her family situation and was shaped most directly by the figures with whom he or she interacted directly: parents, peers, professors, priests (or any other clergy), and politicians.

Now the process of socialization is influenced, to a large degree, by popular culture and the mass media: rock musicians, sports heroes, actors and actresses, and gangs give young people ideas about how to behave, how to dress, how to relate to others, and what to become. There is now a powerful **youth culture** that both uses and is shaped by the mass media, a subculture that has its own media, its own values, its own entertainments (rock music, raves) and is often at odds with what might be described as mainstream (and adult) society.

Television also stimulates and feeds our desire for gossip, caters to our erotic desires (Esslin notes that drama is essentially erotic), and diverts our attention from important considerations. By doing these things it often leads to diminishment or loss of the ability to think logically and make rational decisions. It even affects our political decision making, Esslin (1982) says, because we tend now to focus our attention on the faces of politicians as they respond to questions rather than listening to what they say or thinking about their arguments. That is, we take what we have learned from watching filmed and televised drama and apply it to watching politicians, turning politics into theater—or more into theater, for those skeptics who argue that politics has always had a dramaturgical or theatrical dimension to it.

The celebrated incident in which O.J. Simpson, the famous football player and media celebrity, after allegedly killing his former wife and a young man, raced along the highways in Los Angeles while being chased by police cars and helicopters from television stations shows how we can often blur the distinction between reality and fantasy. This episode, which lasted several hours and was shown on many stations, mesmerized the country. It seemed more like fiction than reality, more like one of the films Simpson had appeared in than real life. It became a gigantic drama and a media event, one that led to all kinds of speculation about the role of the media in the incident, violence and sports, the problem of domestic violence, the true nature of celebrity, and a number of related topics. All of these matters are now part of the national agenda, and it is to this aspect of media effects we now turn.

AGENDA SETTING

The mass media carry programs that focus our attention on certain aspects of life (that they deal with in news shows, talk shows, narratives, and other genres) and, in so doing, so the theorists of **agenda setting** suggest, consign other aspects of life and topics to secondary status or, in some cases, relative obscurity. Advertisers argue that people cannot buy products they have never seen or heard of; in the same light, agenda theorists suggest that people can become concerned only about topics that have been brought to their attention.

It is generally held that the media, and more precisely the texts they carry, do not necessarily tell us how or what to think—though some theorists who believe the media have ideological dimensions argue that the texts they carry shape our thinking. Instead, many media theorists suggest, the media provide a frame of reference and tell us, implicitly, what topics to think about. In determining the subjects we think about, the media set our agendas and ultimately shape our decision making on political and social issues.

In our newspapers and news programs and other programs devoted to public issues, certain matters are given more prominence than others, and this phenomenon provides us with a scale of importance that also has social and political implications. As Maxwell E. McCombs and Donald L. Shaw (1976), two prominent agenda-setting theorists, have written, "Audiences not only learn about public issues and other matters from the media, they also learn how much *importance* to attach to an issue or topic from the emphasis the media put on it" (p. 176). Agenda-setting theorists tend to focus upon news media rather than mass communication in general, but it could be argued that dramatic programs, in dealing with certain subjects and calling them to people's attention, also have an impact on the agenda-setting process.

GATEKEEPERS

The individuals in media organizations who decide what will be shown or written about are often referred to as **gatekeepers.** For newspapers and for radio and television news shows, these gatekeepers determine what the important news is on a given day and the relative prominence the various stories will receive. Research on the gatekeeping function in media goes back to the 1950s, when journalism scholars started investigating the role of newspaper wire editors. It has since expanded to consider the whole process of the selection of events to be dealt with in the news media.

A number of factors affect the decision making of gatekeepers, such as the organizations they work for, the media in which they work (television news needs visual images), and their own socioeconomic status. Selecting topics for inclusion in a day's news show or the daily newspaper is, after all, a subjective matter. What is important to a liberal Democrat may not be important to a conservative Republican, and what is important to a man may not be important to a woman. All of the subcultural and demographic characteristics discussed earlier in this book play a role in the gatekeeping process. We can see a link between gatekeeping and agenda setting. The information that gatekeepers let through their gates becomes the material that sets our agendas.

Chaim Eyal (personal communication, 1994) explains the origins of this theory as follows:

> The research and theory of gatekeeping had originated in the work of Kurt Lewin, who, in 1947, studied processes of decision making with regard to household food purchases. He observed that information always flows along certain channels, which contain "gate areas," where decisions are made. This idea was taken up in 1950 by David Manning White. He studied the processing of information by telegraph wire editors in American newspapers, whose decisions to discard news items coming over the wire were seen as the most significant gatekeeping activity. In 1969, the theory was revisited by A. Z. Bass, who differentiated among different gatekeeping roles. He argued that the most important gatekeeping activity occurs within the news organization, involving two stages, news gathering and news processing. He developed the model shown below:

Stage 1   *Stage 2*
Raw News → *News Gathering* → *News Copy* → *News Processing* → *Completed Product*

writers	editors
reporters	copyreaders
local editors	
translators	

Gatekeeping theory demonstrates to us that the news we get is, in the final analysis, someone's view of what is important news or news that will attract and keep the attention of readers or audiences—not necessarily what is important news. We can also think of news programs' camera shots as gatekeeping, for though they show us images of "reality," what we see reflects someone's decisions about which images to shoot and then use on the air. Thus where there are media, there is always a kind of manipulation going on.

CULTIVATION THEORY

George Gerbner, former dean of the Annenberg School for Communication at the University of Pennsylvania and editor of the *Journal of Communication*, is the theorist most associated with **cultivation theory**. His argument is that television tends to dominate our "symbolic environment" and that the image of reality found in the mass media shapes, to a great degree, the conceptions of reality that media consumers have.

Television, the most dominant medium (in terms of the amount of time people spend with it daily), has something close to a religious dimension to it, and as our primary storyteller, it cultivates or reinforces certain values and beliefs in its viewers. It has more or less usurped the role that used to be played by significant others: peers, priests, professors, parents, and even politicians.

The problem is that the image of the world created by television (and by the media in general) is a very distorted one. In his essay "Liberal Education in the Information Age," published in 1984, Gerbner sketches out the distortions found in the televised image of the world (see Gerbner, 1984/1991). He notes that the world reflected on television is permeated by violence, and that it underrepresents women (men outnumber women by a ratio of three to one), underrepresents older people, is dominated by professional people, and wildly overrepresents cops and criminals. As Gerbner writes:

> What is the world according to television like? To discover its main features and functions, we have to look at familiar structures in an unfamiliar light. Rituals rationalize and serve a social order. They make the necessary and inevitable appear natural and right. In conventional entertainment stories, plots perform that rationalizing function. They provide novelty, diversion, and distraction from the constant reiteration of the functions performed by casting, power, and fate. The main

points to observe, therefore, are who is who (number and characterization of different social types in the cast); who risks and gets what
(power to allocate resources including personal integrity, freedom of
action, and safety); and who comes to what end (fate, or outcomes
inherent in the structure that relates social types to a calculus of power,
risks and relative success or failure). (in Berger, 1988, p. 323)

Heavy viewers of television tend to believe that the world they see
on television is what the real world is like, and this leads to all kinds
of misconceptions. Narratives play an important role in shaping our
views—a notion with which Esslin (1982) would agree. Because
people will not turn their television sets off, Gerbner adds, parents
must learn how to deal with television, and educators must develop
media studies courses that will encourage critical viewing as a means
of countering the negative influences of television (and by implication, much of the material found in the mass media in general).

REINFORCEMENT

One of the most important studies of mass communication under-
taken to date was conducted in the 1940s by sociologist Paul F.
Lazarsfeld and his colleagues, who investigated the role of the media
in political campaigns in general and the voting process in particular
(Lazarsfeld, Berelson, & Gaudet, 1944/1968). These researchers discovered that political campaigns seem to have relatively little impact
on people, and that their basic effect seems to be that of reinforcing
beliefs that people already hold. This reinforcement occurs, in part,
because people tend to be selective in what they watch and read; they
prefer to pay attention to messages that are congruent with what they
already believe. Lazarsfeld et al. also found that people are strongly
affected by group affiliations (a subject I will discuss in Chapter 4),
by personal contact, and by information from opinion leaders. These
individuals tend to be better informed than the ordinary person, tend
to be from elite segments of society, and generally have a relatively
high status. (In some cases they may not recognize that they are
functioning as opinion leaders.)

Lazarsfeld et al.'s research led to the theory of the **two-step flow**
of media. In the first step, the media influence opinion leaders; in the

second step, these opinion leaders influence others with whom they have direct contact in groups of one sort or another. This theory suggests that groups to which individuals belong can have significant impact on their voting behavior. This might be expected, given that people tend to belong to groups that both support and reinforce their belief systems.

The work of J. W. Riley and M. W. Riley (1959) is of interest here. These researchers investigated the role of primary groups and reference groups in the communication process, and they suggest that mass communication is a social process that both influences and is influenced by the social environment. Denis McQuail (1969) explains Riley and Riley's theory:

> They discuss evidence which shows the recipient of communication to be affected by his environment, by his relationship to primary groups, secondary groups and other reference groups, and through these to the wider social structure. At the same time, the communicator "emerges as part of a larger pattern, sending his messages in accordance with the expectations and actions of other persons within the same system." (p. 82)

Riley and Riley, McQuail adds, propose a number of question for exploration. They ask how the communication process fits in with society in general; how the flow of money, people, and goods affects things; and what function the mass communication system performs for the social system as a whole. Their work is useful because it reminds us that mass communication exists in society and both affects and is affected by society.

THE SPIRAL OF SILENCE THEORY

In an article titled "The Spiral of Silence: A Theory of Public Opinion," Elisabeth Noelle-Neumann (1974) argues that people who think they represent a minority point of view tend to keep quiet, whereas those who think they represent a majority point of view tend to make their views known. People, she explains, are afraid of isolating themselves, and if they sense that they hold a minority viewpoint, they tend to doubt their capacity to think correctly. She discusses situations in which there are conflicting positions to be considered, as well as the matter of where a person stands relative to these positions:

> He may find himself on one of two sides. He may discover that he agrees with the prevailing (or winning) view, which boosts his self-confidence and enables him to express himself with an untroubled mind and without any danger of isolation, in conversation, by cutting those who hold different views. Or he may find that the views he holds are losing ground; the more this appears to be so, the more uncertain he will become of himself, and the less he will be inclined to express his opinion. (p. 44)

"Thus," she adds, "the tendency of the one to speak up and the other to be silent starts off a spiraling process which increasingly establishes one opinion as the prevailing one" (p. 44).

This means we must often hold public opinion suspect, because many people will want to be on what they perceive to be the winning side. Noelle-Neumann offers the historical example, and discusses Tocqueville's analysis, of the French Revolution and the church. In this period there was widespread contempt for religion, and the French church, thinking it represented a minority view, fell silent. The people of France, frightened of becoming isolated, joined in the opposition to religion, even though they did not agree with those who opposed the church. Noelle-Neumann cites Tocqueville:

> People still clinging to the old faith were afraid of being the only ones who did so, and as they were more frightened of isolation than of committing an error they joined the masses even though they did not agree with them. In this way, the opinion of only part of the population seemed to be the opinion of all and everybody, and exactly for this reason seemed irresistible to those who were responsible for this deceptive appearance. (p. 45)

People, then, often overestimate the strength of those who oppose their views and underestimate the strength of those who share their views, and are swayed because of their fear of becoming isolated. A process is then set in motion in which those with minority views (or views they believe to be minority views) become increasingly silent lest they become isolated, judged negatively by those holding the majority view.

The spiral of silence theory is a social psychological one that suggests the mass media do not reflect opinion but create it. As Noelle-Neumann writes, "According to the social-psychological mechanism here called the 'spiral of silence,' the mass-media have to be seen as creating public opinion; they provide the environmental pressure in which people respond with alacrity, or with acquiescence, or with silence" (p. 51).

We can even see socialization as being connected, to a certain degree, with the feelings of young people about "fitting in" and doing what is popular or, conversely, being isolated and behaving in a manner so as to avoid this feeling. Noelle-Neumann's theory can be seen as an example of the sociological maxim that people behave according to their perceptions of the world, not according to the way the world actually is (to the extent that we can know this, that is).

The mass media, then, through processes already described, such as gatekeeping and agenda setting, more or less create the public opinion to which people respond—by acquiescing or becoming silent. But a look at the American political landscape in recent years makes one question whether the spiral of silence theory is correct. We have any number of competing minority voices and groups of all kinds, from gays to feminists to African Americans and members of other ethnic cultures, that have not been silenced as this theory suggests they should be. Instead, they are making themselves heard more and more and, in the process of doing so, are having an impact on American public opinion and the political process. On the other hand, the current movement for political correctness does tend to muffle the voices of some individuals and groups who might be considered part of the "silent majority," and this effect is somewhat close to the theory of the spiral of silence. Whether this so-called silent majority has been silenced by fear of being isolated or chooses to remain silent is not quite clear.

CULTURAL IMPERIALISM

Noel-Neumann's theory is a conservative one, and it is similar to theories of mass society that were popular 50 years ago. There is a different theory that comes from the left, from Marxists and critical communications scholars, that concerns the impacts that mediated texts have on people—a theory known as **media imperialism** or **cultural imperialism.** This theory asserts that media texts produced in Western nations have come to dominate media channels all over the world. It costs a great deal to produce television shows, for example, but it is relatively inexpensive to show them on television networks, so Third World countries broadcast television shows (and other countries as well) that are made, for the most part, in the United States and Western Europe.

According to the theory of cultural imperialism, these television programs (and other mass media as well, such as films, records, and even comic books) destroy native cultures and enculturate people in Third World countries with American and Western European culture; further, they carry ideological messages that subtly brainwash Third World peoples into accepting American and Western European bourgeois capitalist values and beliefs.

As an example of this kind of thinking, let us consider one of the more celebrated studies, Ariel Dorfman and Armand Mattelart's *How to Read Donald Duck: Imperialist Ideology in the Disney Comic* (1975, 1991), which attacks Disney and Disney comics for spreading bourgeois imperialist **ideology.** The authors contend that this form of imperialism is particularly pernicious because those who read Disney comics, in Latin America and, by extension, elsewhere, do not recognize that they are being thus indoctrinated. The people who read comics detailing the adventures of Donald Duck and other Disney characters are also learning to believe in those characters' values and worldview. The indoctrination is tied to the narratives and the ways the comic characters relate to work, the social structure, science, technology, the future, and so on. For example, Disney's comic-book writers make use of common stereotypes of various Latin Americans, and this serves to separate groups from one another, thus making them more susceptible to indoctrination by the mass media:

> Our Latin American countries become trash cans being constantly
> repainted for the voyeuristic and orgiastic pleasures of the metropoli-
> tan nations. Every day, this very minute, television, radio, magazines,
> newspapers, cartoons, newscasts, films, clothing, and records, from the
> dignified gab of history textbooks to the trivia of daily conversation, all
> contribute to weakening the international solidarity of the oppressed.
> We Latin Americans are separated from each other by the vision we
> have acquired of each other via the comics and the other mass culture
> media. This vision is nothing less than our own reduced and distorted
> image. (Dorfman & Mattelart, 1975, p. 55)

There are a great many data available that show how media flow
or are diffused from America, Western Europe, and a few other
countries to other, essentially Third World, countries. The question
is whether the dominant mass-mediated culture is destroying native
cultures and indoctrinating people with Western bourgeois ideology. This process take place, cultural imperialism theorists argue,
even though those who create the texts carried by the media may not
consciously inject ideology into their texts. The process is an auto-
matic one, for the most part. People who have been raised in bourgeois capitalist societies do not recognize the degree to which they
have absorbed this ideology, and without recognizing what they are
doing, they pass their beliefs on to others.

One problem with this theory is that it assumes that all individuals
decode texts the same way, and that they "get" the message, even
though they are not aware they are doing so. Semioticians have
suggested that when it comes to the mass media, **aberrant decoding**
is the norm, so individuals may not be "reading" texts in the ways
cultural imperialists think they are. In a similar vein, **reader-response**
theorists have suggested that all texts are ultimately brought into
existence, so to speak, by their readers. So we have to wonder
whether the ideological messages that cultural imperialism theorists
find in texts are actually getting through to readers and viewers and
manipulating them. Cultural imperialism theory rests, ultimately, on
the idea that media effects are powerful. However, as I have suggested, there is good reason to question this assumption.

The concerns of many people in Third World countries, as well as
those of others in First and Second World countries, led to the idea
of a "new world information order" to monitor the flow of informa-

tion (and entertainment, popular culture, and so on) throughout the world. In 1980, UNESCO published the McBride Report, which recommended that journalists should have free access to all news sources, that censorship should be abolished everywhere, and that commercial influences on communications should be limited (McBride et al., 1980)—recommendations that some citizens of some Third World countries found unpalatable.

WHAT THE RESEARCH SHOWS

William J. McGuire (1988, 1991), a psychologist at Yale University, has made a massive study of research on media effects and has come to the conclusion that a belief in "large media effects" cannot be supported. He discusses research on a variety of subjects related to media effects:

> Evidence in support of the claim that the media have sizable direct impact on the public is weak as regards each of the dozen most often-mentioned intended or unintended effects of the media. The most commonly mentioned intended effects include: (1) the influence of commercial advertising on buying behavior; (2) the impact of mass media political campaigns on voting; (3) public service announcements' efficacy in promoting beneficial behavior; (4) the role of prolonged multimedia campaigns in changing lifestyles; (5) monolithic indoctrination effects on ideology; and (6) the effects of mass-mediated ritual displays on maintaining social control. The most often cited unintended effects of the mass media include: (1) the impact of program violence on viewers' antisocial aggression; (2) representation on the media as a determinant of social visibility; (3) biased presentation of media as influencing the public's stereotyping of groups; (4) effects of erotic materials on objectionable sexual behavior; (5) modes of media presentation as affecting cognitive styles; and (6) the impact of introducing new media on public thought processes. (p. 274)

In the article quoted above, which is a condensation of a much longer one titled "The Myth of Massive Media Impact: Savagings and Salvagings" (1986), McGuire surveys the research that has been done on media effects. He argues that although we all have gut feelings, so to speak, that the media have powerful effects, nobody has been able to prove that such is the case. It may be that we lack the methodologies to prove effects, or that in searching for general effects we miss circumscribed effects or in looking for direct effects we miss indirect effects. Whatever the case, according to McGuire, there is very little empirical support for the theory that the media are powerful. He concludes, "For the present, a Scotch verdict of 'not proven' seems indicated on the proposition that the mass media have vast direct impacts on the public exposed to them" (1988, p. 389). We should keep McGuire's research in mind when we talk about the powerful effects of the mass media. Those who talk about such effects are often those who have vested interests in this theory: advertising agencies and academics who do research in the mass media and are dependent on grants to fund their research.

It may also be that we are asking the wrong questions. Instead of focusing our attention on the media per se, perhaps we should think about the impacts on people of specific mass-mediated texts. Were there no significant effects of the television broadcasts of the videotape of the Rodney King beating? Or of the handshake between Arafat and Rabin at the White House? Does a great film (or, for that matter, a great novel or a great play) have no effects? It may be that we should narrow our focus and consider individual texts and the ways they may be affecting individuals and groups and societies, rather than always focusing on the media in general. It may be more useful to employ humanistic methods to investigate texts, rather than social scientific ones, which have a number of inadequacies—as McGuire points out. Finally, it may be that we want to generalize too much; when we are profoundly affected by a text, we may assume that many others "must be" affected as we are. The matter of media effects remains something of a puzzlement; intuitively, we feel the media must have profound effects, but we cannot prove it.

Ownership of the Mass Media

There is a dilemma we face in discussing the ownership of the media. If the media have **limited effects**, as some argue, then the fact that a small number of people control the media is relatively unimportant. But why would people advertise in the media and waste their money? The media make money by selling advertising space and time, and they do that by promising to deliver the right audiences to advertisers. If the media have limited effects, those with products and services to sell are wasting a great deal of money on advertising agencies and on buying time and space in the media.

It may be best to assume that the media have major effects but that we simply have not been able to figure out how to prove or measure these effects. If that is the case, then the matter of media ownership becomes a very significant matter. Ben Bagdikian (1985) has explored the subject of media ownership in a number of publications; he offers some startling statistics:

> In 1982, fifty corporations controlled half or more of all mass media output. My informal calculation is that this number had shrunk to less than 44 in 1984. The trend in newspaper ownership is a specific example. In 1900, there were 2,042 daily papers with 2,023 different owners. By 1982, there were 760 owners, but 20 of these were corporations that had more than half the business. By 1984, as mergers and acquisitions continued, the 20 had been reduced to 14. (p. 100)

Bagdikian (1988) has argued, in other work, that although there are 2,500 publishers of books, 11 of those publishers have the lion's share of the sales, and that although there are something like 8,000 radio stations in the country, there are only a dozen formats that dominate radio programming, so there is relatively little diversity on the radio in most places. Michael Parenti makes the same argument in his book *Inventing Reality* (1986):

> Freedom of the press, A. J. Liebling once said, is for those who own the presses. Who specifically owns the mass media in the United States? Ten business and financial corporations control the three major television and radio networks (NBC, CBS, ABC), 34 subsidiary television stations, 201 cable TV systems, 62 radio stations, 20 record companies, 59 newspapers including the *New York Times,* the *Washington Post,* the *Wall Street Journal,* and the *Los Angeles Times,* 41 book publishers, and various motion picture companies like Columbia Pictures and Twentieth Century Fox. (p. 27)

And, Parenti points out, the pattern is one that involves increasing concentration of ownership in fewer and fewer hands. Since Parenti's book was published in 1986, the media industry has become even more concentrated, and giant international media megacorporations have developed. The industry is best described as characterized by oligopoly—domination by a few individuals and corporations who have common interests.

It has been estimated that, in the near future, perhaps 500 cable television channels will be available to consumers; however, as in radio, there will be only a limited number of genres or program types shown on these channels, so there will not be as much diversity as we might imagine. And the media conglomerates are waging battles to buy film companies so they will have films to show on many of these channels—it is much cheaper to show a film than to produce a television program.

This process of consolidation of control leads to even greater **cultural homogenization** or standardization of media content, which is particularly dangerous, Bagdikian (1988) argues, because our media tend to be organized on the local level, and we do not have serious national newspapers that can give people a sense of perspective, except, perhaps, for the *New York Times, USA Today,* and the *Wall Street Journal.* In most cities, for example, there is only one newspaper—with, in effect, a monopoly on the news. Something like 95% of all chain newspapers have no competition (Bagdikian, 1988, p. 487). Of course this is balanced, one might argue, by broadcast and cable television news and other sources, but in many cases the newspapers and television stations are part of the same media conglomerates. And in any case, there are just a few media conglomerates controlling most of the media, so if we are not getting our news from one giant media conglomerate, chances are we are getting it from another.

The airwaves, we must remember, are public property, leased to media organizations to be used in the public interest. We must wonder whether the various media conglomerates are actually using the airwaves in the public interest. If, as some theorists argue, the media do set our agendas, and if the owners and editors controlling newspapers, radio stations, television stations, and book publishers do function as gatekeepers, then the fact that a small group of people control the media, a group small enough to fit into one room, is cause for considerable concern.

The problem is not that there is a conspiracy among the various media moguls to brainwash the American public. Rather, the problem is that the owners of the various media empires tend to be from the same **socioeconomic class** and thus tend to have certain interests in common, certain ideological beliefs and political identifications that they tend to share, even though their companies may be competing with one another. This means that stories, texts, films, and shows supporting competing beliefs and ideologies tend to be neglected or downplayed by the dominant media, even though there are some counterculture media.

The Problem of Violence

George Gerbner has studied the amount of violence on television for many years, and each year he comes up with a figure to indicate the amount of violence—or, more precisely, the number of violent acts per hour—on television (see Gerbner, 1984/1991). His figures indicate that a typical hour on television has many acts of violence

in it. There is, of course, the methodological question of how one defines violence; if one's definition is broad, including violent intent and comic violence, one will count many more incidents of violence on television than if one's definition is narrow and highly restrictive, limited to actual portrayals of noncomic violence.

There is a split among media scholars about the effects of televised violence on viewers. Some minimize the importance of mediated violence, arguing that it functions as a cathartic agent and helps individuals to relieve stress and rid themselves of violent feelings in a harmless manner, by watching others be violent. Other scholars argue that violence on television (and in the media in general) has negative effects, that it leads individuals to be violent, to use violence as a means of dealing with problems, to imitate characters who use violence, and to underestimate the effects of violence on others.

Nancy Signorelli and George Gerbner (1988) have created an annotated bibliography of studies of violence that contains brief descriptions of more than 780 articles from scholarly journals and books as well as articles from popular journals, government reports, and conference papers on violence in the media; the areas covered include media content, media effects, pornography and the media, and terrorism and the media.

They explain their definition of media violence:

> Reliable observation and systematic analysis usually requires limited and objective definitions. Most research studies have defined media violence as the depiction of overt physical action that hurts or kills or threatens to do so. A terroristic act is typically defined as one involving violence by, among, or against states or other authorities in order to spread fear and make a statement, usually political. Media violence and terror are closely related. They depict social relationships and the use of force to control, dominate, provoke, or annihilate. By demonstrating who can get away with what against whom, factual and fictional representations of violence or terror can intimidate people; provoke resistance, aggression, or repression; and cultivate a sense of relative strength and vulnerability as they portray the social "pecking order." (p. xi)

Signorelli and Gerbner cite a number of studies that detail the amount of violence found on television (such as one by Bradley Greenberg and others with data revealing that if violence is defined as "physical aggression," it occurs more than 9 times per hour between 9:00 and 11:00 p.m. and on Saturday mornings, during children's programs, more than 21 times per hour).

Signorelli and Gerbner spell out their understanding of *cultivation*, suggesting that, "for most viewers, television's mean and dangerous world tends to cultivate a sense of relative danger, mistrust, dependence, and—despite its supposedly 'entertaining' nature—alienation and gloom" (p. xviii). They note that various researchers, working independently of Gerbner and his associates, have made a number of interesting observations regarding media violence (p. xviii). A few of the main points made by these researchers are as follows:

1. Media exposure to violence boosts public estimates of crime and violence.
2. There is a significant relationship between exposure to crime shows on television and approval of police brutality and bias against civil liberties.
3. Television viewing is related to feelings of anxiety and fear of victimization.
4. Television viewing tends to cultivate the presumption of guilt rather than the presumption of innocence of a suspect.

There is good reason to argue, as the above material suggests, that television violence is not a harmless cathartic but has, instead, very profound effects upon viewers and society in general. Television is, obviously, not the direct cause of much of the violence that pervades U.S. society, but it may be more of a contributing factor than some have imagined.

It is often pointed out that there is violence in much elite literature and in many elite art forms. The body count in *Hamlet* is considerable, but it is relatively minor when compared with those in some particularly violent films, such as *Terminator 2*. However, as a rule, people do not go to the movies seven times a week, whereas many do see the equivalent (as Esslin, 1982, informs us) of seven plays a week in the course of their normal television viewing. And the violence in the elite arts is much more restrained and far less gratuitous than the violence in our television programs, films, and other mass-mediated texts.

As a final point in this discussion, I would like to say something about the complexities we face in dealing with the concept of violence itself. As the great Swiss linguist Ferdinand de Saussure (1966) has pointed out, terms have no meaning in themselves, but derive their meaning from opposing terms in the system in which they are embedded: "Concepts are purely differential and defined not by their positive content but negatively by their relations with other terms of the system" (p. 117). Thus "the most precise characteristic [of these concepts] is in being what the others are not" (p. 117). With

Saussure's admonition in mind, let us consider the possibilities when it comes to aspects of violence. Table 3.4 lists a number of polar oppositions that reflect various kinds of violence. We can see from this list that violence is an exceedingly complicated matter, and that our responses to violence (and the effects violence might have on us) are tied to such matters as whether the violence is defensive, whether it is just part of the scheme of things (as in sports), and whether it is institutionally generated.

Our responses to violence are tied to context (the situation in which it occurs), but the impact of violence on our psyches is more or less the same whether the violence is real, as in the case of wars, or fictive, as in the various stories we watch on television and see at the movies. If that is the case, and many researchers believe it is, then we must be mindful of the potential effects of media violence on ourselves and particularly on children.

Gerbner's theory, it should be pointed out, has been attacked on a number of fronts. Some scholars feel his definition of violence is too comprehensive, so that his data suggest there is more violence on television than is actually the case. Others argue that although Gerbner has been able to document the amount of violence on television, he has not been able to show, demonstrate, or prove (whichever term you prefer) that this violence actually has negative effects on viewers. Content analysis can give us information about the amount of violence on television, some social scientists suggest, but it cannot prove that there is a causal connection between the amount of violence on television and the behavior of people who see this violence. Other social scientists, I should point out, disagree; they argue that we can now show that televised violence does lead to increased violence in the real world. This topic, as I have noted, is the subject of continual and heated debate in the academic community—but, so far, no actual violence (that I know of, that is).

The Neglected Matter of Media Aesthetics

One of the problems with the research done by many mass communication scholars is that it does not consider the impact of **aesthetics** in shaping texts and affecting audiences. For example, quantitative

TABLE 3.4 Polar Oppositions and Violence

mediated violence	violence seen directly
real mediated violence (wars)	fictive mediated violence
comic violence	serious violence
intended violence	actualized violence
violence to individuals	violence to groups
inferred violence	documented violence
police violence (just)	criminal violence
verbal violence	physical violence
violence to humans	violence to animals
"fake" violence (wrestling)	"true" violence (bar brawl)
violence against heroes	violence against villains
violence against women	violence against men
violence in past	violence in future
violence by human agents	violence by mechanical agents
defensive violence	offensive violence
violence by children	violence by adults
weak violence (insults)	strong violence (murder)
accidental violence	intentional violence
visual images of violence	prose descriptions of violence
violence by the insane	violence by the sane
violence as means to end	violence as an end in itself
causes of violence	effects of violence
violence as action	violence as reaction
many minor acts of violence	one major act of violence
violence as emotional response	violence as rational decision
violence against others	violence against self
violence ordered by others	violence decided by self
focus on root causes	focus on triggering mechanisms
sign of depravity	cry for help
violence caused by fear	violence caused by hatred
institutional violence	individual violence
violence as instinctive	violence as cultural
violence as integral (sports)	violence as extraordinary

studies that simply tally the number of violent incidents in a text may miss something important, for it is often the case that one violent image in a narrative text, or one violent scene, has much more power and resonance than others. The way a scene is shot—the cutting, the editing, the use of music and sound effects, the lighting, the camera work—conveys a great deal of information and gives a sense of the importance of what we are seeing relative to other images and events in the text. This kind of thing is hard to quantify, however, so when we count the number of violent incidents in a text, we tend to give them all the same weight.

Let me offer a hypothetical case. Imagine a western program in which there are four fistfights between the hero and various henchmen of the main villain. At the end of the show, there is the classic gun battle between the villain and the hero, in which the hero shoots the villain and kills him. The gun battle is the center of dramatic interest and leads to the resolution of the story, but if we quantify the violence simply according to the number of violent incidents, we get five violent incidents. That number is correct, but it does not do justice to the text.

The reason we neglect the weight of various violent incidents in a text is that we do not know how to rate their relative importance. We have not yet figured out how to quantify qualitative matters. We can classify violent acts according to the kind of violence (fights, attempted killings, killings, and so on), but that still does not do justice to the aesthetic elements in a text.

Below, I discuss in turn some of the more important elements of media aesthetics as they apply to television (and, by implication, film and other media as well).

Use of lighting. Lighting affects our understanding of what is going on in the text, and can make us feel certain things.

Use of color. Colors trigger emotional responses—the gunslinger in black, the cowboy hero in white, and so on.

Use of camera shots. Camera shots are "cues" that tell us, indirectly, how to respond to the images we see. Different shots have different meanings, and as we watch television we learn what various shots mean. Because television has a small screen, relative to films, there is extensive use of close-ups and most of the action tends to be on the z-axis—the axis that stretches vertically from the eye to the screen and then to the horizon. This means that the medium of television has a profound effect on the way television narratives and other texts are shot. A close-up, for example, tells us that we are to examine the expression on a performer's face, to see how he or she reacts to

TABLE 3.5 Meanings of Shots and Camera Work

	Definition	*Meaning*
Shot		
close-up	small part of body	intimacy
extreme close-up	very small part of body	inspection
medium shot	most of body	personal relations
full shot	all of body	social relations
long shot	setting and characters	context, scope
z-axis	vertical action toward viewer	involvement
wipe	image wiped off screen	imposed end
dissolve	image dissolves into next one	weaker ending
Camera work		
pan down	camera looks down on X	power of viewer
pan up	camera looks up at X	weakness of viewer
dolly in	camera moves in	observation
fade in	image appears on screen	beginning
fade out	image disappears from screen	ending
cut	switch from one image to next	excitement

something or what he or she may be thinking (Esslin, 1982). A long shot, on the other hand, establishes context and gives us a sense of setting and place. A zoom shot, when the camera lens brings us closer and closer to some situation, suggests the need to inspect what is going on and, by implication, that something important is taking place. When the camera pans up, so that we are looking up at someone, a certain sensibility is created that is quite different from when the camera pans down, and we find ourselves looking down on someone. (See Table 3.5 for further examples.)

Editing style. Quick cutting between shots creates a sense of excitement in viewers; they work in a way opposite to that of lingering shots, which slow things down. Editing involves the sequencing of shots; through editing, elements of a text can be intensified or clarified. The editing used in televised professional football games, where we often see a single play from three or four different perspectives, is very avant-garde—it gives viewers a particular sense of history and time, namely, that time is cyclical and things repeat themselves. It also suggests that there are a number of different ways to see the same thing, much as *Rashomon* does.

Film editors play a major role in shaping the emotional responses of audiences. Editors are often called upon to work "miracles" (as the wife of a film editor I know describes her husband's labors) in transforming a chaotic collection of scenes, shot by undisciplined directors, into some kind of a coherent whole.

Use of sound and music. Sound and music add energy and help establish mood. Sound effects give texts an element of verisimilitude, and music establishes a mood and provides the audience with stimuli that shape its responses to the events going on in the text.

Other elements. There are also traditional literary criticism aspects to keep in mind when we deal with narrative—the quality of the writing, the theme of the text, its plot, the characterization, the quality of the performances, and many other matters as well. And, as Esslin (1982) points out, many nonfiction texts on television are dramatized or, by the use of aesthetic elements, given a dramatic quality.

Readers who are interested in pursuing the area of media aesthetics further may want to consult Herbert Zettl's *Sight-Sound-Motion* (1990) or my book *Seeing Is Believing* (1989). There are also many other books available that deal with lighting, sound, and other aspects of media aesthetics and visual communication in general.

SUMMARY

This chapter has focused upon the role of media in mass communication. We began with a discussion of different theories of media, and then considered Marshall McLuhan's theory that "the medium is the message" and his description of different media as hot or cool. Next, a number of theories dealing with media effects were presented, including analyses of the dramatic aspects of mediated texts, agenda setting, gatekeepers, cultivation theory, reinforcement, the spiral of silence theory, and cultural imperialism. The chapter then addressed research that suggests the hypothesis of strong media effects cannot be proven. A discussion of the matter of media ownership and the roles of media conglomerates came next, followed by discussion of the ongoing debate over the issue of violence in the media. The chapter ended with a brief consideration of media aesthetics.

At eight p.m. eastern standard time on the evening of October 30, 1938, Orson Welles with an innocent little group of actors took his place before the microphone in a New York studio of the Columbia Broadcasting System. He carried with him Howard Koch's freely adapted version of H. G. Wells's imaginative novel, War of the Worlds. *He also brought to the scene his unusual dramatic talent. With script and talent the actors hoped to entertain their listeners for an hour with an incredible, old-fashioned story appropriate for Hallowe'en.*

Much to their surprise the actors learned that the series of news bulletins they had issued describing an invasion from Mars had been believed by thousands of people throughout the country. For a few horrible hours people from Maine to California thought that hideous monsters armed with death rays were destroying all armed resistance sent against them; that there was simply no escape from disaster; that the end of the world was near. Newspapers the following morning spoke of the "tidal wave of terror that had swept the nation." It was clear that a panic of national proportions had occurred.

Hadley Cantril, *The Invasion From Mars*, 1966

CHAPTER 4

THE AUDIENCE

There are, as we have seen, a number of conflicting theories about the effects of media, but media need audiences to have effects. Is there a "mass" audience of alienated and separated individuals who are susceptible to indoctrination and brainwashing, or do members of an audience have the power to subvert messages brought to them by the mass media and use them for their own purposes? In this chapter I begin with a discussion of cultures and subcultures in the United States. I then consider Erik Erikson's ideas about life cycles and the crises individuals face at each stage in their development. I use Erikson's theory to offer some personal hypotheses about music and television addiction. This leads to a discussion of political cultures and the roles they may play in affecting our choice of texts. Next, I offer an explanation of uses and gratifications theory, along with a list of some of the more important uses and gratifications associated with media use. I follow this with an examination of functionalism, aberrant decoding, Basil Bernstein's work on socioeconomic class and codes, and the work done by marketers to segment audiences into smaller groupings for the purpose of selling them products and services. Audiences are seen as part of larger entities, namely, societies—and it is to this subject we turn after our discussion of audiences.

When we think of audiences, we tend to lump everyone listening to a television show or a radio program into one homogeneous group, but as anyone who spends much time listening to the radio knows, audiences are made up of a variety of different groups of people—which is why there are so many different kinds of radio stations.

Radio is now a medium that narrowcasts—each station aims its programs at particular segments of the audience who like certain kinds of music or talk shows or whatever. Television, on the other hand, remains essentially a **broadcast** medium, in the sense that it aims for larger audiences, even though much television is carried by cable and other new technologies such as satellites and, soon, our phone lines. (A considerable amount of local television programming, often carried by cable, does narrowcast; that is, it seeks specific audiences.) The industry is currently in flux, and as new technologies develop, it is evident that some marriage of computers, telephone transmission lines, film, and television will take place.

Masses Versus Publics

Audiences are not "masses" that are composed of individuals all of whom are separated from one another, who have little in common, and who can easily be brainwashed by those who control the media and determine what texts will be made available to people. I have yet to find a "mass man" or "mass woman" who fits the descriptions offered, on the basis of theory rather than fact, by some scholars who write about the media and the so-called masses.

Instead of talking about masses, it makes more sense, I would argue, to talk about **publics.** Publics are groups of people who form themselves into audiences for specific texts offered on the various media. The term *mass*, as I pointed out earlier, has many negative connotations and projects an image of individuals and audiences that does not do justice to their variety and powers of discrimination. Sandra J. Ball-Rokeach and Muriel G. Cantor (1986) expand on the notion that audiences should not be presumed to be "mass consumers":

> From our point of view, the media audience is not to be understood as mere consumers who passively accept anything that the media offer,

but as active individuals and members of social groupings who consume media products in the context of their personal and social goals. In modern societies, that means quite a lot. Because the media system plays such an important role in society, linking the audience to all its various institutions, it is necessarily the case that the media will play important social and personal roles in individual and collective life. (pp. 17-18)

This would suggest that the idea that audiences are masses does not hold up to scrutiny. Audiences are made up of various groupings who come together, so to speak, to consume mediated texts, for a variety of reasons. There is no unified mass audience for television, and the programs television brings to the public, via broadcasting and cable and satellite, are more diverse than many critics recognize.

Cultures and Subcultures in the United States

Let's take the United States as an example. There may be certain basic values and beliefs that link all Americans together, but the fact is that there are numerous geographic regions within this country as well, and people's beliefs, values, and even their accents can vary from region to region. Each part of this country—from the East Coast, to the Midwest, to the Deep South, the Southwest, and the Pacific Northwest—has its own character, culture, even cuisine. A look at the numerous conferences in college football shows this diversity.

We also have subregions, such as California within the West, and sub-subregions, such as Northern California and Southern California, that have their own distinctive qualities. Within these, there are urban, suburban, and rural areas that have their own qualities. In California, for example, there are big cultural differences between San Francisco and Los Angeles, and within each of these cities there are also areas that have their own characteristics. In San Francisco, for instance, Pacific Heights, the Castro, and the Mission District all have their own identities. Table 4.1 shows the different levels we should consider when analyzing audiences in a society as diverse as that in the United States. In urban areas, for example, marketing research indicates that people with similar incomes, values, and lifestyles tend to live in the same sections of the city, though this is

TABLE 4.1 Levels of Analysis for Audiences

Category	Example
National	United States
Regional	West
Subregional	California
Urban	San Francisco
District	The Castro, the Mission, Pacific Heights
Street	Union Street, Pacific Avenue, Clement Street

not always the case. Even within a city there are many different districts, as Table 4.1 suggests.

Theorists of mass culture have tended to downplay the significance of the numerous **subcultures** that exist in a given society. In addition, they have neglected, to varying degrees, the roles that factors such as age, gender, sexual orientation, race, political values, religion, ethnicity, education, and occupation play in the scheme of things. We see how these factors play out in the radio industry, where we have stations now that cater to every kind of person living in a city, and the same can be said about magazines and books. Some magazines, such as *Wired*, are now available electronically on the Internet; this kind of thing is happening more and more often. In the San Francisco Bay Area, for example, one can find (or could find at one time) all of the following kinds of radio stations: "beautiful music," Mexican Top 40, news/sports/traffic and weather, black soul, Christian, country, classical, news talk, adult contemporary, big bands, light rock, Top 40, all oldies, soft jazz/blues/salsa/reggae, progressive alternative, easy listening, free form, jazz fusion, album-oriented rock, and punk/new wave. Clearly, there is incredible variety available on radio, and stations are changing their formats all the time (from classical music to talk shows, from Top 40 to Spanish language, and so on) and new formats are being invented as well.

Erik Erikson, Life Cycles, and Station Preferences

Let's consider the role that age plays in media usage. I became acutely aware of this when I invited the vice president of an easy-

TABLE 4.2 Erikson's Life-Cycle Crises

Stage	Crisis
Infancy	trust versus mistrust
Early childhood	autonomy versus shame and doubt
Childhood	initiative versus guilt
School age	industry versus inferiority
Adolescence	identity versus identity confusion
Early adulthood	intimacy versus isolation
Middle age	generativity versus stagnation
Old age	integrity versus despair

listening radio station to talk to one of my classes. When my students, who were then in their late teens and early 20s, heard what station he came from, they laughed. "That's all right," my speaker said, "because when you are in your 30s and 40s you'll be listening to *my* station, and I'll have the last laugh." What my guest was pointing out is that as people get older, their tastes often change, and they "migrate" from one kind of station to another. Erik Erikson (1968) discusses the "crises" that, according to his theory, all people pass through in the course of their development from birth to old age. There are, he says, eight stages that all of us must negotiate, and at each stage we are confronted with an existential dilemma—a choice we must make that will either lead us in the direction of continued growth and maturation or bring negative consequences upon us.

We are faced, Erikson says, at each stage of our lives with a crisis that we must resolve before we can move on to the next stage of our development, and we never reach a point where do not have some crisis to face and triumph over. Table 4.2 lists Erikson's eight stages of development and the specific crisis that exists at each stage. Most people, according to Erikson's theory, are able to deal with each crisis, but there are individuals who cannot master some of them. The failure to master a crisis at an early age complicates a person's life and makes it difficult for him or her to master crises faced at a later stage in development.

Erikson's discussion of these crises is quite lengthy, for each stage of development is quite complicated and the crises are equally complex. Each crisis involves an opposition—different routes one can take in the process of development. As an example of Erikson's analysis, consider his comments about people of school age and adolescence, periods when media usage is very important:

> If an unlimited imagination as to what one might become is the heritage of the play age, then the adolescent's willingness to put his trust in those peers and leading, or misleading, elders who will give imaginative, if not illusory, scope to his aspirations is only too obvious. By the same token, he objects violently to all "pedantic" limitations of self-images and will be ready to settle by loud accusation all his guiltiness over the excessiveness of his ambition. Finally, if the desire to make something work, and to make it work well, is the gain of the school age, then the choice of an occupation assumes a significance beyond the question of remuneration and status. (p. 129)

According to Erikson, the problems that adolescents face involve primarily the "diffusion" of identity, the inability to find a strong, coherent, focused sense of self—especially as it relates to occupation. This might explain why a given teenager, with his or her particular problems and crises to master, listens to a certain radio station, reads certain books, attends certain films, and watches certain television shows. We can use Erikson's crises to understand better the choices people make, at different ages, in their media consumption. But age is only one factor. We have to add to it many of the other matters mentioned above, which why it is so difficult to make sense of people's media consumption. Rather than a huge, undifferentiated mass of people in an audience, we find ourselves, a good deal of the time, moving closer to the other extreme—hyperindividualism and anarchy. (A case in point: It is now possible to order custom-made tapes, with the musical selections you want, in the order that you want them. Could this signify the end of the album as we know it?)

A Hypothesis on Taste in Music

From Erikson's theory, I have gained an insight that has led me to a hypothesis I would like to present about why some young people like rock music and other "chaotic" styles. (I define *hypothesis* as an informed guess, based on some concept or theory, that helps us better understand some phenomenon.) If young people have problems with identity, they may choose rock music and other similar kinds of music because in a way it renders their psychological chaos, caused by identify diffusion problems, invisible. That is, this music functions as a kind of camouflage. It also expresses rebellious, anti-authoritarian feelings, and, when played extremely loud, can be used to irritate parents and others. Later, when young people have grown older and have firmed up their identities, they no longer need such music to "hide" their identity problems, so they can move on to other kinds of music, such as light rock or easy listening or golden oldies.

A Hypothesis on Heavy Television Use and Addiction

Let me offer one other age-related hypothesis—one that deals with heavy television use and television addiction. (I first formulated this hypothesis in the mid-1970s; the discussion that follows is based on my article "Fear of Feeling: Vicious Cycles in Videoland and the Real World," 1977.) This hypothesis draws on the work of two psychiatrists, Herbert Hendin and Julius E. Heuscher. Hendin (1975) noticed in some research he was doing in the early 1970s that many young people were trying to live emotion-free lives and were replacing emotional relationships with accumulated "fragmented sensory experiences" through drugs.

Heuscher makes an important point in his book *A Psychiatric Study of Myths and Fairy Tales* (1974). Folktales, he notes, emphasize the

importance of the harmonious development of individuals and are tied
to the age levels of those listening to the tales. The situation is different
when it comes to television, however. Children can see on television too
many of the conflicts of adult life, and thus can be pushed prematurely
into the world of grown-ups. Such children tend to become afraid of
growing up and can be stunted in their maturation. Heuscher comments
on the relation between television viewing and fear of growing up in
children who have seen dramas too adult for them, though he cautions
that this has not been demonstrated by research:

> The changes in values and behavior, the increased passivity and the
> lack of wholehearted and lasting commitments among the young (and
> not so young), are undoubtedly due to numerous factors among which
> television has not been established as the essential one. However, we
> cannot remain complacent and let things drift along until demonstra-
> ble, permanent, serious side effects are undermining the health of the
> population.

The theory of vicious cycles works as follows, then:

1. In some people, childhood and other television viewing leads to fear
   of becoming adults and being involved in adult conflicts.
2. This fear of becoming adults leads, in turn, to the incapacity to sustain
   wholehearted emotional relationships.
3. This incapacity, in turn, leads to fear of marriage, nonrelational sex,
   fear of feeling, and so on.
4. This kind of behavior is unsatisfying to those involved and leads to
   anxiety, pain, and escapism of various kinds, such as drugs or television viewing, to obtain "relief."
5. Television watching becomes, for such people, a narcotic upon which
   they are dependent to escape from their imprisonment within themselves—to have vicarious experiences, to have mediated "relationships" with others, and so on. At the same time television provides
   relief, however, it reinforces latent childhood fears, thus helping create
   the very dependencies these viewers use it to escape from, making
   them, in a sense, "prisoners" of their television sets and, ultimately, of
   themselves.

All of this starts, I suggest, because young children are exposed to
dramas on television that are too adult for them, and this leads

ultimately to their being caught up in a vicious cycle—becoming dependent on the very thing that created their problems. Obviously, this is a somewhat simplistic argument, but it is a beginning step in explaining why some people are so dependent on television and watch so much.

Aaron Wildavsky's Theory of Political Cultures

I have noted above the existence in the United States of numerous groups and subcultures (what have also been called "taste cultures" when related to popular culture and the mass media). Using the work of Aaron Wildavsky, who was, until his untimely death in 1993, a professor of political science at the University of California at Berkeley, I would like to explore the role played by political values and beliefs

		Strength of Group Boundaries	
		Weak	*Strong*
Number and Variety of Prescriptions	*Many and Varied*	Fatalists	Elitists
	Few and Similar	Individualists	Egalitarians

Figure 4.1. Wildavsky's Model of Four Political Cultures

in the choices people make among mediated texts. According to Wildavsky (1989), social and cultural matters play an important part in determining our preferences:

> The dimensions of cultural theory are based on answers to two questions: Who am I? and What shall I do? The question of identity may be answered by saying that individuals belong to a strong group, a collective that makes decisions binding on all members or that their ties to others are weak in that their choices only bind themselves. The question of action is answered by responding that the individual is subject to many or few prescriptions, a free spirit or a spirit tightly constrained. The strength or weakness of group boundaries and the numerous or few, varied or similar prescriptions binding or freeing individuals are the components of their culture. (p. 25)

From these two questions and the possible answers to them, Wildavsky argues that we can derive four **political cultures,** made up of hierarchical elitists, competitive individualists, egalitarians, and fatalists. In the course of developing his theory, Wildavsky changed the names he used for these groups from time to time; he even noted a fifth group, hermits, but this relatively small group is not important to this discussion. Wildavsky's groups are shown in Figure 4.1, which is based on his adaptation of the work of British social anthropologist Mary Douglas, with whom he sometimes collaborated.

Wildavsky (1989) shows how the combination of rules and group boundaries leads to the formation of the four political cultures as follows:

> Strong groups with numerous prescriptions that vary with social roles combine to form hierarchical collectivism. Strong groups whose mem-

bers follow few prescriptions form an egalitarian culture, a shared life of voluntary consent without coercion or inequality. Competitive individualism joins few prescriptions with weak group boundaries, thereby encouraging ever new combinations. When groups are weak and prescriptions are strong—so that decisions are made for them by people on the outside—the controlled culture is fatalistic. (p. 26)

Wildavsky deals with a number of issues relevant to these groups that concern political scientists, but my concern here is with the implications the existence of these four political cultures has for the study of mass communication. Our preferences, according to Wildavsky's theory, are not just a matter of individual taste, but are rooted in our social groups and the political beliefs connected to them. A person who is a hierarchical elitist, who believes in the importance of stratification, would, in principle, find it difficult to enjoy a text that is egalitarian in nature and that stresses what people have in common (needs) rather than what separates them. This is because, generally speaking, we seek to avoid the cognitive dissonance caused by entertaining ideas that conflict with those we already hold; rather, we seek reinforcement of our beliefs, ideas that support and justify them.

An individual is not locked in to any one political culture, however; if a person is not getting the payoffs expected, he or she will sometimes change from one political culture to another (in some cases, people are forced to make such changes). Thus people in one political culture who are considering a move to a different political culture might watch a television program or go to a film that may persuade them to make a change.

I often play a game with my students. After I explain Wildavsky's theory about political cultures, I ask them to figure out what films, television programs, songs, games, sports, magazines, and newspapers the members within each political culture would be expected to like. Table 4.3 displays some of the choices some of my students have proposed in a number of classroom exercises.

I should point out that there is no one simple explanation for why people watch the television shows they do, go to the films they do, read the books they do, and so on. That is why it is reasonable to suggest that personal tastes are not the only factor involved in media

TABLE 4.3 Political Culture and Media Preferences

Topic Analyzed	Hierarchical Elitists	Competitive Individualists	Egalitarians	Fatalists
Songs	"God Save the Queen"	"My Way"	"We Are the World"	"Anarchy in the U.K."
Television shows	The MacNeil/ Lehrer Newshour	Dynasty	The Waltons	The A-Team
Films	Top Gun; The Right Stuff	The Color of Money	Woodstock	Rambo
Magazines	Architectural Digest	Money	Mother Jones	Soldier of Fortune
Books	The Prince	Looking Out for Number One	I'm Okay, You're Okay	1984
Heroes	Ronald Reagan	Lee Iacocca	Mohandas Gandhi	Jim Jones
Heroines	Queen Elizabeth II	Mary Kay	Mother Teresa	Madonna
Games	chess	Monopoly	new games	Russian roulette
Sports	football; polo	tennis (singles)	Frisbee	Roller Derby; professional wrestling
Fashion	uniforms	three-piece suits	jeans	thrift-store clothing

preferences—personal tastes, it turns out, are not as personal or idiosyncratic as we might imagine.

Jonathan Edwards, a Puritan minister and philosopher, argued in the early 1600s that we can act as we please, but we cannot please as we please. He was trying to reconcile his belief in free will with his belief in God's being all-powerful, so he separated action from belief and argued that what pleases us comes from God. Wildavsky has argued that what pleases us is derived from our social groups and our political cultures. Both make what is essentially the same argument: We do things that please us (in the realm of action), but why these things please us (in the realm of choice) is another matter. Sigmund Freud, who believed that many of the things we do are tied to sexual urges and unconscious imperatives, has also made a similar argument.

Uses and Gratifications

Much of the research in mass communication and the mass media has come from scholars with a social psychological orientation who have focused on the effects the media have on people and have investigated the role of the media in attitude formation, attitude change, and so on. Other scholars have concerned themselves with something else, namely, the uses to which people put the media—more precisely, the texts carried by the media—and the gratifications they get from these texts. This theory of media utilization became popular a number of years ago; in recent years, it has been somewhat eclipsed by other views, though there are still a number of researchers who use it in their work. Chaim Eyal (personal communication, 1994) points out that uses and gratifications theory can be said to stem from the work of Raymond Bauer in the 1960s:

> The work of Raymond A. Bauer is very important to mention in this context. His article "The Obstinate Audience: The Influence Process from the Point of View of Social Communication" was originally published in the *American Psychologist*, . . . 1964. . . . The significance of Bauer's ideas is in both what he had to say and the timing of his thoughts, relative to the then prevailing notion of media effects. Bauer suggested (this was a novel idea at the time) that, contrary to the prevailing conceptualization, media audiences are active, purposive, and goal directed in their media-seeking and media-use behavior. Recall that the accepted notion of media effects at the time was the null—or minimal—effects concept, coupled with a view of audiences as passive and impressionable. Bauer offered the idea that people turn to, and use, the mass media and media content to satisfy certain needs and desires. Bauer suggested that people are selective and relate to their media consumption as an exchange, which they enter with certain expectations, anticipating to fulfill those expectations. Audiences exercise initiative, free will, and independence. The uses and gratifications tradition was founded upon Bauer's ideas and took off from where Bauer left off.

This notion, that audiences are not passive but selective, and are tied to various groups seeking certain kinds of gratifications, has been mentioned previously in this chapter. The discussion of uses and gratifications that follows expands on this notion.

Katz, Blumler, and Gurevitch (1979) explain the uses and gratifi-cations perspective in more detail, mentioning some work by early researchers in the area:

> Herzog (1942) on quiz programs and the gratifications derived from listening to soap operas. Suchman (1942) on the motives for getting interested in serious music on radio; Wolfe and Fiske (1949) on the development of children's interest in comics; Berelson (1949) on the functions of newspaper reading; and so on. Each of these investigations came up with a list of functions served either by some specific contents or by the medium in question: to match one's wits against others, to get information or advice for daily living, to provide a framework for one's day, to prepare oneself culturally for the demands of upward mobility, or to be reassured about the dignity and usefulness of one's role. (p. 215)

These studies suggest that people use texts for varying purposes and regard these texts as functional for them. Uses and gratifications theory implies that members of an audience are active and selective in choosing certain texts (or genres) that provide them with various gratifications.

There is some question about how active people are in their media usage and how selective they are in choosing mass-mediated texts, for there is also some evidence to suggest that in some cases televi-sion viewers watch whatever is on—sometimes not even bothering to change channels once the set is turned on. On the other hand, we know that the development of remote control devices has led to a good deal of "zapping" and channel cruising, as some viewers create, so to speak, their own programs—collages made of pieces of television programs being broadcast at particular moments in time. And the development of new cable and satellite systems that will be capable of providing hundreds of different channels also suggests that viewers are selective—when, that is, there are significant choices open to them.

The uses to which people put mass-mediated texts and the gratifications they derive from those texts are quite varied. The following list of such uses and gratifications is based on the suggestions of a number of scholars (this list is based on a table in my book *Media Analysis Techniques*, 1991; in that text, each of the uses and gratifications is discussed in some detail):

- to be amused
- to see authority figures exalted or deflated
- to experience the beautiful
- to have shared experiences with others
- to satisfy curiosity and be informed
- to identify with the deity and the divine plan
- to find distraction and diversion
- to experience empathy
- to experience, in a guilt-free situation, extreme emotions
- to find models to imitate
- to gain an identity
- to gain information about the world
- to reinforce belief in justice
- to believe in romantic love
- to believe in magic, the marvelous, and the miraculous
- to see others make mistakes
- to see order imposed upon the world
- to participate in history (vicariously)
- to be purged of unpleasant emotions
- to obtain outlets for sexual drives in a guilt-free context
- to explore taboo subjects with impunity
- to experience the ugly
- to affirm moral, spiritual, and cultural values
- to see villains in action

Looking at this list, we can better understand why certain texts appeal to certain individuals and, by extension, to large numbers of people. The theory of uses and gratifications suggests that our media usage is not mindless; there are reasons, even though we may not be conscious of them or able to articulate them, behind the text choices we make.

A number of theorists now argue that individuals use the media in their own ways to resist forces of domination and control coming from government agencies or those who control the media. This point is made clearly in the subtitle of a book on humor edited by two British scholars, Chris Powell and George E. C. Paton, *Humour in Society: Resistance and Control* (1988).

Some people, when asked about why they watch television or listen to the radio, say they do it "to kill time." From the uses and gratifications perspective, killing time would be a use of the media, but the matter is more complicated. Why do people kill time by watching a soap opera rather than a news program, or a ball game rather than a documentary? The answer, I would suggest, is that there are other unrecognized or unconscious uses and gratifications that affect our text choices.

Functional Analysis

Given that we have been investigating uses and gratifications, a **functional** approach to mass communication, it makes sense here to say something about functionalism in general, a theory that is the source of considerable debate and argumentation among social scientists. The functional approach argues that a phenomenon or institution, such as mass communication, should be analyzed in terms of its contribution to the maintenance of the system in which it is found—in the case of mass communication, that would be society in general.

There are a number of different aspects to functional theory. Let us take an institution (and society in general) as the subject of our analysis. If an institution contributes to the maintenance of the society in which it is found, that institution would be described as functional. If the institution contributes to the breakdown of the

TABLE 4.4 Aspects of Functionalism

Aspect	Example
Functional	food: helps keep the body going
Dysfunctional	poison: kills the body
Nonfunctional	appendix: plays no known role in maintaining body
Manifest function	go to meeting of political organization to work to win election
Latent function	go to meeting of political organization to look for sexual partner (with similar political views)
Functional alternative	professional football as functional alternative to church on Sundays

society in which it is found, that institution would be described as **dysfunctional.** If the institution plays no role in maintaining or breaking down (that is, has no effect on) the society in which it is found, it would be described as **nonfunctional.** The matter is complicated because in some cases an institution may be functional in certain respects and dysfunctional in others.

In addition, in some cases the effects of an institution are obvious and intended. We describe this as the **manifest function** of the institution. In other cases, the effects of an institution are hidden or not recognized. This we describe as the **latent function** of the institution. Finally, in some cases other institutions take over the functions of a given institution. An institution that assumes the functions of another is described as a **functional alternative.**

Table 4.4 lists the various aspects of functionalism and provides some examples. We can see that there are many different aspects to functionalism, a topic that has been at the center of much social scientific thought (and controversy) over the years. It is reasonable to think about our institutions and the things we do (including media usage) in terms of their functions, and to suggest that we are not aware of the "real" reasons we do some things. Functional theory has been attacked by some scholars, who argue that it is conservative and static—focusing on maintaining systems rather than on changing them. In addition, it has been difficult to find institutions that are functional for entire societies.

This latter notion is at the heart of the problem. Thompson, Ellis, and Wildavsky (1990) suggest a way of resolving the difficulties posed by functional theory:

> Another charge commonly leveled against functional explanation is that it commits one to an ideologically conservative perspective—that by showing a behavior's purpose one is therefore predisposed against changing it. Though past functionalists may have often pursued a conservative agenda, our contention is that functional explanation per se is ideologically neutral. . . . Our theory improves upon traditional functional explanations in another important way. Dating back to Comte, functionalists have sought functional requisites that are valid for all social systems. What interests Comte, Radcliffe-Brown, and Parsons [famous functionalist thinkers] is what *all* social systems must do to survive. The result of this search was a banal list of (largely definitional) functions that every system must perform. It is not very illuminating to say, as Parsons does, that a "functional imperative" of every society is that it be integrated, i.e., have a means for regulating internal conflicts. . . . Cultural-functional analysis pursues what we believe is a more fruitful tack of asking how types of social relations vary in the resources they can employ to resolve internal conflicts. (p. 107)

As these authors point out, earlier functionalists assumed that behavior that was functional for some individuals and groups in a society had to be functional for everyone, which neglected conflict. Their theory, they argue, by tying functions to the four political cultures, addresses conflict. This is so because it deals with who benefits from a given pattern of behavior, which may be functional for one way of life or group but dysfunctional for another.

Functional theory, we see, can operate at several levels. On the highest level, looking at society at large, functional theory would try to determine whether mass communication, in general, is functional or dysfunctional, what its manifest and latent functions might be, and whether it is a functional alternative to something else. Wildavsky and his colleagues argue that analyses on this level tend to be very abstract and do not lead to very interesting results.

On an intermediate level, we can consider the functions served by mass media for a group or a given segment of society. Is there a difference, we might ask, between the functions of the mass media for those who own them and for those who are their audiences? Those who own and control the media may have an agenda of their own and may not care about the social impacts of the texts they carry. The matter of violence in the media is a case in point. Does this violence have latent functions that may be destructive? Do audiences in general and individual members of audiences in particular have any rights as far as media content is concerned? The media, after all, are carried on airwaves "owned" by the public.

On the most immediate level, we can consider the uses individuals make of mass communication and, in particular, mass-mediated texts, and the gratifications people seek from these texts. We can ask individuals about why they like certain programs and gain a good deal of information about how they "use" the media. And each of us can consider the uses and gratifications we seek from texts carried by the various media and how these texts may be affecting us and our loved ones.

The Problem of Aberrant Decoding

There is yet another complication involved in our understanding of the role of audiences relative to the process of mass communication and media usage in particular. In Chapter 1, I sketched out a general theory of communication advanced by Roman Jakobson that involves a sender and a receiver of messages (or, as some put it, an addresser and an addressee). The sender encodes a message and the receiver decodes it. That is, senders use combinations of language, light, sound, color, and various other techniques to put their messages into some form in which receivers will "get" the message and understand what is being communicated.

In conversation, we use words, intonation, pacing, redundancy, and facial expression to send our messages. Even in something as seemingly simple as a conversation, we find there are often misunderstandings by the receiver of the sender's messages. For example, if someone says something to another person in an ironic tone, but that person does not "catch" the irony, the message will be misunderstood.

When communication is taking place through an art form more complicated than conversation, such as film or television, the chances for misunderstanding and misinterpretation between receivers (audiences) and senders (artists) are much greater. Texts of all kinds are complex, and films and television programs—which use lighting, sound, music, images, and performance elements—are extremely complicated. Thus it is not unreasonable to expect that some members of audiences will make mistakes in decoding the messages being sent in these texts. Umberto Eco (1984), the distinguished semiotician, has suggested that we call this "aberrant decoding," which he says "is the rule in the mass media" (p. 106). By this he means that individuals generally do not decode texts in the ways that those who create them want them decoded, because people bring different educational levels, backgrounds, interests, and so on to each text. He notes, "Codes and subcodes are applied to the message [text] in the light of a general framework of cultural references, which constitutes the receiver's patrimony of knowledge: his ideological, ethical, religious standpoints, his psychological attitudes, his tastes, his value systems, etc." (p. 115).

Eco offers the example of foreigners in strange countries who do not understand the **codes,** the allusions and references speakers make, and so on. This problem of aberrant decoding becomes very significant with the development of the mass media, especially because there are generally big differences in class levels and education (and related matters) between the writers and creators of the texts and the people who receive them.

If individuals tend to decode the texts carried on the media aberrantly, the question must be raised as to whether these texts can perform the ideological functions that some critics claim they do. Marxist critics, critical theorists, and others suggest that the texts carried on the media are imbued with ideological content that is used to "brainwash" (to put it crudely) the "masses" so that the dominant classes can maintain their status.

On the other side of the spectrum, advertising agencies claim that their commercials successfully persuade huge numbers of people to buy this brand of soda pop or that brand of deodorant. It is difficult to support the notion of powerful media effects if people who watch texts carried by the media are misinterpreting the messages being sent and decoding these texts aberrantly. (Advertising agencies sometimes find themselves in a curious position. When called upon to testify before government agencies, they argue that commercials cannot shape behavior, yet they tell those who manufacture products and provide services that commercials can persuade people to buy their products and services.)

The Media and Attitudes

The media in general, and commercials in particular, play a role, then, in shaping our attitudinal structure. Our **attitudes,** which are defined by social psychologists as "states of mental preparedness or readiness," are connected to our past experiences and can influence particular behaviors. As Davison, Boylan, and Yu (1976) point out, attitudes of audiences are connected to a number of different considerations:

> First, there are personality and educational differences; some people are more easily persuaded than others, some can understand more complicated arguments, and so on. Second, people are situated in a variety of social settings; one person's friends and family may be liberal, while another is in a more conservative milieu. Third, the attitudes that any one person has may vary in strength; he or she may be deeply committed to a given church or political party, may be more loosely attached, or may have no attitudes at all on some political and religious subjects. Fourth, external events may affect audience attitudes; a communication that is not very persuasive in peacetime may be quite compelling in time of war—or vice versa. (p. 174)

Thus a number of variables affect our attitudes, so that it is difficult to say that a given communication will lead to a given behavior. We may be able to find a correlation—Communication X was followed by Behavior Y—but that is not the same as finding causation: Communication X caused Behavior Y.

Attitudinal theory suggests that advertising works with people's preexisting tendencies, beliefs, and dispositions and attempts to sound a "responsive chord," to use Tony Schwartz's (1974) term, rather than to create an entirely new piece of music, so to speak.

TABLE 4.5 Elaborated and Restricted Codes

Elaborated Code	Restricted Code
users aware of code	users unaware of code
middle and upper classes	working classes
complex use of grammar	simple use of grammar
varied vocabulary	uniform vocabulary
sentence structure complex	sentence structure simple (short, repetitious sentences)
careful use of adjectives and adverbs	little use of adjectives and adverbs
high-level conceptualization	low-level conceptualization
logical	emotional
much use of qualification	little use of qualification

Socioeconomic Aspects of Decoding

The decoding of messages is done by individuals, but it is influenced by those individuals' socioeconomic classes. That, at least, is the argument of Basil Bernstein (1977), a prominent English sociolinguist who suggests that members of the British working classes learn codes that are different from those learned by members of the British middle and upper classes. His research has led him to claim that British children learn either an "elaborated" code (found in the middle and upper classes) or a "restricted" code (found in the working classes). These two codes are illustrated in Table 4.5.

Bernstein suggests that use of the restricted code has some positive aspects—for example, users of the restricted code often communicate warmth and kindness—but the general consequences of its use are negative. Use of the restricted code fosters a kind of present-mindedness and other attitudes that play an important role in hindering those living in poverty from escaping it. This is because language acts as a prism through which we see the world, and, as social scientists have suggested, we act on the basis of our perceptions of the world, which are often far removed from the way things really are.

Sociologists tell us that thought is, to a considerable degree, socially determined. That is, it is shaped in large measure by matters such as race, religion, socioeconomic class, political culture, and geographic location. Language and the way we decode messages and texts are greatly influenced by these factors. It is difficult for many

Americans, with our strong belief in individualism, to accept that many of our ideas are tied to our social situations, but even the concept of individualism is something we learn at some time—we are not born valuing our individuality. What is of interest is the role mass communication plays in this process.

Durkheim on Collective Representations

The great French sociologist Émile Durkheim deals with the role of **collective representations** in his classic work *The Elementary Forms of Religious Life* (1967). The relationship that exists between our thoughts and ideas and these collective representations is very complicated. As Durkheim argues in an often-quoted passage:

> Collective representations are the result of an immense co-operation, which stretches out not only into space but into time as well: to make them, a multitude of minds have associated, united, and combined their ideas and sentiments; for them, long generations have accumulated their experience and their knowledge. A special intellectual activity is therefore concentrated in them which is infinitely richer and complexer than that of the individual. From that one can understand how the reason has been able to go beyond the limits of empirical knowledge. It does not owe this to any vague mysterious virtue but simply to the fact that, according to the well-known formula, man is double. There are two beings in him: an individual being which has its foundation in the organism and the circle of whose activities is therefore strictly limited, and a social being, which represents the highest reality in the intellectual and moral order that we can know by observation—I mean society. This duality of our nature has as its consequence in the practical order, the irreducibility of reason to individual experience. In so far as he belongs to society, the individual transcends himself, both when he thinks and when he acts. (p. 29)

This is a long and complicated quotation, but it is a very significant one, for it is one of the more eloquent explanations we have of how it is that human beings can be brought up in societies, yet still have the element of individual thought in them. There is, Durkheim tells us, a duality found in human beings: We are animals with certain physical needs and drives, and we are also social beings; as such, we are affected in profound ways by being members of societies—or, more important for our purposes, groups within societies.

Durkheim's statement leads me to suggest that we must consider the biological, psychological, and social aspects of men and women when trying to make sense of their behavior. We cannot reduce behavior to social and political factors alone, or to psychological ones or to biological ones. How we determine which of these might be dominant in a given situation is a problem that cannot be solved generally, but has to be worked out on a case-by-case basis.

Reception Theory

Reception theory (or reader-response theory) makes a distinction between the "artistic" nature of the text and the "aesthetic" realization or interpretation of the text by the reader (or viewer or listener if we consider film, television, and recorded music, for example). The artistic aspect of the text involves the work created by the writer or artist or whoever might be responsible for generating the text. But this text, as we have seen, really is full of possibilities for varying interpretations and does not come into being, so to speak, until it is realized by the person reading or seeing or listening to it. As Wolfgang Iser (1988), one of the leading proponents of this theory, writes:

> The text as such offers different "schematized views" through which the subject matter of the work can come to light, but the actual bringing to light is an action of *Konkretisation*. If this is so, then the literary work has two poles, which we might call the artistic and the aesthetic: the artistic refers to the text created by the author, and the aesthetic to the realization accomplished by the reader. From this polarity it follows that the literary work cannot be completely identical with the text, or with the realization of the text, but in fact must lie halfway between the two. The work is more than the text, for the text only takes on life when it is realized and furthermore the realization is by no means independent of the individual disposition of the reader—though this in turn is acted upon by the different patterns of the text. (p. 212)

Iser's position, then, is that there is a role for the reader and this role is an important one, for the reader brings the text into existence and both reader and the text affect each other (see Table 4.6).

TABLE 4.6 The Reader-Text Relationship

Text	Work	Reader
author		reader, audience
artistic plane		aesthetic plane
sender		receiver
creates a text		realizes the text

This position is the polar opposite of the now discredited **hypodermic needle theory** of media, which asserted, in essence, that everyone in an audience reads and is affected by a given text the same way. This theory was connected to theories of mass societies and mass culture held by some media sociologists. It does not seem reasonable to argue that everyone gets the same message, but some theorists argue that there are "preferred" readings, ones that the creators of texts want people to get, that critics of texts can discern, and that most people get—or should be able to get.

It seems reasonable to suggest that although every reader interprets a given text on the basis of his or her background and social situation (race, religion, socioeconomic class, and so on), and thus all readings are different, there still must be a considerable amount of agreement among members of an audience about what texts mean. Otherwise, communication, except on the most basic level, would not be possible. We all help "realize" every text we read, but we also probably find some kind of common core in these texts when we read them. This matter, of how people read texts, is also the subject of considerable debate among mass communication researchers.

Audience Segmentation by Marketers

One way marketers have tried to solve the problem of discordant readings is by finding "microaudiences," groups of people who share similar **demographics** (personal characteristics such as age, income, class, gender, place of residence, and marital status) and thus might be expected to "read" texts—in particular, print advertisements and radio and television commercials—in somewhat similar manners.

TABLE 4.7 The VALS Typology

Group	Characteristics
Survivors	poor, old, depressed
Sustainers	relatively young, crafty, on edge of poverty
Belongers	conventional, unexperimental
Emulators	ambitious, upwardly mobile, status conscious
Achievers	leaders of society, efficient, well-to-do, materialistic
I-am-me's	young, narcissistic, impulsive
Experientials	older I-am-me's seeking experiences and inner growth
Societally conscious	simple living, support environmentalism
Integrateds	mature, tolerant, self-assured

One of the more interesting attempts to segment audiences is the VALS (Values and Life Styles) **typology** developed by SRI International, which categorizes consumers in terms of their values and lifestyles rather than their vital statistics. SRI researchers have isolated nine distinctive types of consumers on the basis of values and lifestyles; they argue that advertisers should pitch their advertisements and commercials specifically to each of these groups, though there is some overlap among them.

The nine groups in the VALS typology are listed in Table 4.7, which also shows important characteristics of each group. The theory is that when one is advertising a particular product or service, it makes sense to focus one's appeals on the values and beliefs of the particular segment of the population that is most likely to be interested in the product or service. For example, Merrill Lynch's famous "Bullish on America" campaign did not have the desired results because it appealed to "belongers" (the herd of bulls) when it should have been directed toward "achievers," the group most likely to invest in stocks and bonds. The campaign was altered and a new theme, "a breed apart," was used, which was more congruent with the values of achievers.

The VALS typology is but one of numerous means of dividing the American public—or, from our perspective, American audiences—into groups so that advertisers can create texts that will reach them better. Let me offer one other example. A recent *New York Times* article reported on a survey conducted by a marketing research firm,

TABLE 4.8 Lifestyle Groups and Magazine Choices

Group	Magazines Read
Home engineers	*Family Circle, Good Housekeeping*
Real guys	*Popular Mechanics, Mechanix Illustrated*
Ethnic PEWNEPs[a]	*Ebony, Essence, Jet*
Information grazers	*People, Time, Bon Appetit*
Armchair adventurers	*Reader's Digest, Modern Maturity, Travel & Leisure*

NOTE: a. PEWNEPs are "people who need people."

Yankelovich Partners, that showed that the magazines people read can be a more accurate guide to their consumer behavior than such traditional demographic factors as residence, age, and marital status (Elliott, 1993). The Yankelovich Partners researchers developed a typology consisting of five categories, or "media communes" (see Table 4.8). Each of these groups tends to watch certain television shows, to vote in certain ways, to have a particular annual income range, and to buy certain kinds of products. The theory is, of course, that if you are advertising a certain product, you have to know who your audience is and what it is like—so members of the audience will "read" your commercials correctly and be most susceptible to their appeals.

The typology is not perfect because some people read magazines that, logically speaking, they should not read, according to the researchers. But it does indicate the relationship that exists between what people read and their lives in general. The same kind of thing has been done for zip codes; where people live has a major impact on their consumption patterns.

Implicit in all the groupings that market researchers develop is the notion that there are various groups, clusters, or subcultures of people who have different values, beliefs, lifestyles, demographics, and psychographics, and—ultimately—that one cannot expect the entire audience to read and be affected by a text the same way. The existence of these various typologies is an ironic commentary on theories of mass society that argue people are more or less all the same and can be manipulated easily by the mass media.

SUMMARY

In this chapter we have discussed various theories relating to the role of audiences in the process of mass communication. Topics considered have included mass culture theories, Erikson's work on the stages of development, my hypotheses on the ways different age groups use and are affected by the mass media, Aaron Wildavsky's work on political cultures, and the role these political cultures play in our choice of texts carried by the mass media. We have also considered the uses people make of texts and the gratifications they get from them, the roles that attitudes play, and the problems caused by aberrant decoding of texts. In addition, we have addressed the role of readers in the creation of "works" from texts and have examined various typologies developed by market researchers to divide the American public into groups with specific attributes—to avoid the problem of aberrant decoding and to facilitate marketing products to them by identifying their distinctive characteristics.

I suggest that America is actually made up of a number of taste cultures, each with its own art, literature, music, and so forth, which differ mainly in that they express different aesthetic standards. . . . The underlying assumption of this analysis is that all taste cultures are of equal worth. . . . Because taste cultures reflect the class and particularly education attributes of their publics, low culture is as valid for poorly educated Americans as high culture is for well-educated ones, even if the higher cultures are, in the abstract, better or more comprehensive than the lower cultures. This principle suggests two policy alternatives: (1) "cultural mobility," which would provide every American with the economic and educational prerequisites for choosing high culture; and (2) "subcultural programming," which encourages all taste cultures, high or low. I opt for subcultural programming.

Herbert Gans, *Popular Culture and High Culture*, 1974

CHAPTER 5

AMERICA/SOCIETY

This chapter on society and the media deals with a number of topics of a sociological nature—in the broadest sense of the term. The discussion addresses systems of mass communication, some of the functions of mass communication (such as surveillance, integration, entertainment, the ensuring of cultural continuity, and mobilization), and a number of the common criticisms of mass media and mass communication (i.e., that the media lead to fragmentation, escapism, addiction, cultural homogenization, privatization, and stereotyped thinking, among other things)—some people blame everything that goes wrong on television, the medium "we love to hate." On the other hand, some theorists argue that people use the media in an emancipatory manner, to resist domination, surveillance, and so on. Some Russian jokes serve as examples of the use of humor in the media as a means of resisting Communist brainwashing. The discussion then moves on to the topic of the differences between critical and administrative forms of research on mass communication. This is followed by some definitions of the concept of postmodernism and an assessment of its impact on people's lives. This discussion, which is concerned with styles of art, is preparation for the final chapter, which deals with artists and the creative process.

When we think about the process of mass communication, it is important that we consider not only the role mass communication plays in society and the effects the media have on individuals and society (so-called media effects), but the effects society has on mass communication and the media. Remember that, as I am using the term, *mass communication* refers to a process of spreading messages, texts, and so on to large audiences through the use of the media. There are a number of different arrangements possible relative to the role of the government and the mass communication media.

Four Systems of Mass Communication

In their classic study *Four Theories of the Press*, Fred Siebert, Theodore Peterson, and Wilbur Schramm suggest that there are four main systems of mass communication (or were as of 1963, when their book was published):

1. the Soviet Communist system
2. the libertarian system
3. the social responsibility system
4. the authoritarian system

In the following discussion I modify their ideas slightly, because things have changed considerably since 1963. I also should point out that some scholars argue there are many different systems that could be set up; this list of four is used only as a means of showing some of the more important ones.

First, there is the system that used to be found in the Soviet Union and other Communist countries (and is still found, to a degree, in the People's Republic of China). This system allowed the Communist Party to operate or control the media and to use them to indoctrinate the public with Communist principles and ideas. The government ran the media and used them to spread what we could call propaganda (Marxist-Leninist ideology), to convince people of the efficiency and legitimacy of the government.

We have to wonder how effective this media control was, given that the people in Communist countries kicked out the Communists as soon as they recognized that the Russian Army would not be invading. This, after 50 years of media indoctrination (another example supporting the theory that media have weak effects).

The second system, the libertarian (a term with a somewhat different meaning nowadays, when we have a Libertarian Party), allows for so-called free media, in which private corporations are allowed to control channels and operate networks under the supervision of various government agencies. This is the situation found in the United States and in many Western European countries, where government-run networks no longer have a monopoly on the airwaves.

The third system is also found in the United States and other countries with "free" media, but the focus is on the social responsibility of those who own and control the media of mass communication. In the United States there is a continual battle being waged by those supporting the libertarian view of media (corporations that would like to be completely free to maximize their profits) and those supporting the social responsibility view of media (academics and others who fear that the media are irresponsible and are not being used in the public's interest).

The fourth group, the authoritarian, is for all intents and purposes a stronger version of the Soviet Communist model, and exists in countries where strong dictators can exercise virtually absolute control of the media; North Korea, the "hermit state" as it is sometimes called, is an example. The spread of new technologies in recent years has made it very difficult for those in power in such countries to maintain control of the media. In many areas of China, for example, viewers can pick up networks from Hong Kong and other free countries, so they can watch news shows that give them much more accurate information about what is going on in the world than their own programs deliver. They can also watch other kinds of programs broadcast from outside China. Some theorists believe that the West German television shows East Germans were able to see were a factor in the ultimate breakdown of authority in East Germany and the reunification of Germany. These programs exposed East Germans to a consumer culture in West Germany that many East Germans (and those in other Soviet satellites) longed for.

Those Who Pay the Piper Call the Tune

When we think about the various focal points to be considered in analyzing mass communication, the fact that in the United States we have allowed the media to be dominated by private corporations must be given great weight. The public owns the rights to the airwaves (or spectrum, which is limited) and, in principle, allows private corporations to use them in the public's interest. Whether or not the media conglomerates, the networks, the newspaper chains, the radio networks, and so on are doing so is the subject of a great deal of controversy, because those who pay the piper call the tune.

Many critics of our system of mass communication argue that the search for private profit gets in the way of the public good, and this need to make profits is what is behind the considerable (some would say excessive) commercialization of the media and the amount of violence and sexual exploitation found in many television programs and films. In our system, the owners of the media must deliver audiences to advertisers. In their quest to get the largest audiences possible for their shows (with the right **psychographics,** or psychological similarities, and demographics, of course), so as to maximize profits, the people who own and run the media will go to any lengths.

The fact that we have the system of mass communication we have in the United States is, one might say, an accident. It is tied to our history, our national character, our belief in free-enterprise capitalism, our basic values, and a number of other variables. We could have had a much different system—one in which the government determines, in large measure, what programs will be made and played on the radio or shown on television. There are certain benefits from such arrangements, but also certain costs or problems connected with having the government run the mass media.

If the government operates the mass media and can control what people see, hear, and read, it can use the media for propaganda purposes. On the other hand, it is increasingly difficult to shut out media texts that are beamed down from satellites, broadcast over shortwave systems, transported on audio- or videotapes, or printed on secret presses. In principle, to look at the positive side of things, governments can protect viewers from excessive media violence, sexual exploitation, and commercialization. Governments can also control the amount of

TABLE 5.1 Functions of Mass Communication and Their Results

Function	*Result*
surveillance	inspection
integration and correlation	interpretation
entertainment and play	pleasure
cultural continuity	socialization
mobilization	unification

television that is broadcast, which has the effect of saving television addicts from themselves—at least as far as broadcast, cable, and satellite television are concerned. Television addicts can, of course, use their VCRs to watch tapes and get their video fixes that way.

Some Social Functions of Mass Communication

In Chapter 4, I offered some discussion of the theory of functionalism and the matter of whether functional theory is useful. I quoted Thompson, Ellis, and Wildavsky (1990), who argue that functionalism still is a concept of central importance, but we must not look for high-level functions that apply to every aspect of society. Instead, we should focus our attention on what might be described as middle-range functions, the functions of particular institutions and the roles these institutions play in society. Thompson and his colleagues also suggest that functionalism is not conservative or static and can deal with change and conflict.

With these points in mind, let us consider some of the more important functions of mass communication in society. This discussion is based on the ideas of Harold Lasswell, Charles R. Wright, and a number of others who have addressed this subject in various publications (I modify the terms these scholars have used slightly in Table 5.1).

SURVEILLANCE

Some scholars theorize that media serve a surveillance function: People use mass communication to keep in touch with what is going on in society, to make sure they are not surprised by something that might be important to them. This involves everything from finding out about the traffic and the weather to keeping track of local, national, and international events, such as politics, wars, and natural disasters. The term *surveillance* suggests an element of anxiety that pushes people to be attentive to what is going on around them. The more alienated we feel, the more separated we feel from others (in large metropolitan areas this happens a great deal); the more danger-ous we feel society is, the more we rely on the surveillance function of mass communication.

INTEGRATION AND CORRELATION

Media serve an integration and correlation function in that they help people to organize and try to make sense of what they learn through mass communication. If surveillance gives us data, integra-tion and correlation help us to interpret these data and to connect them to our interests and everyday lives. Some of this organization is done by the people who operate the mass media, and some of it is done by individuals, who are **selectively attentive**; that is, people generally focus their attention on topics that interest them and ne-glect a great deal of other information.

ENTERTAINMENT AND PLAY

William Stephenson (1967/1988) argues that the central function of mass communication is to help people entertain themselves; he opens *The Play Theory of Mass Communication* with this statement: "It is the thesis of this book that at its best mass communication allows people to become absorbed in *subjective play*" (p. 1). According to Stephenson, too much of the focus of mass communication research has been on effects and the role mass communication has (or may have) in shaping people's opinions and attitudes. What is missing, he suggests, has been any concern with mass communication's en-tertainment functions—its play elements.

There can be no question that entertainment is one of the most impor-tant functions of mass communication media. It is not easy, however, to try to separate information from entertainment, because information can be entertaining and entertainment can be informative. Perhaps the best way to deal with this complication is to suggest that in some cases entertainment is the primary function and information is of secondary importance, whereas in other cases just the opposite is true. (In recent years we have begun to describe some programs as "infotainment," indicating that they merge informational and entertainment functions.)

Local news programs are supposed to be informative; that should be their primary function. But many of them, with their focus on murders and other violent crimes, fires, and celebrities, have very strong entertainment aspects to them. Local news programs also devote a considerable amount of time to covering sports, which is a form of entertainment, and in some cases to obvious entertainment matters, such as film and restaurant reviews. The reason local news programs focus on entertainment so much is that they have become profit centers for local television stations instead of functioning as services to the community, as they did in the past.

CULTURAL CONTINUITY

We use the term **popular culture** to refer to a whole range of phenomena, many of which are connected to mass communication. Many critics suggest that the larger the audience (that is, the more popular a show is), the lower the quality of the show must be—to appeal to some mythical "lowest common denominator." I suggest that we can talk about the "largest common denominator" just as well. *Popular culture,* as I understand the term, refers to the texts carried by the mass media and to a large range of nonmediated activities, interests, and behaviors—though these behaviors may be indirectly connected to the media. I am talking here about fads, fashions, and other forms of collective behavior.

Many critics have focused all their attention on the word *popular* and have neglected the *culture* part of popular culture, although it is an important element. Anthropologists use the term *culture* in many different ways, but it usually involves, among other things, the transmission of a people's beliefs, values, and practices from one generation to another.

Sociologists, as pointed out earlier, use the term *socialization* to describe the process by which individuals are taught the rules and roles and mores they need to function in a given group or society. Anthropologists talk about *enculturation*, which is similar to socialization in that both concern the transmission of information from one generation to another. It can be argued, then, that mass communication plays an important role in keeping cultures and subcultures alive. By showing people what others do, mass communication affects social and cultural practices; in many cases, it leads to their modification. These modifications may help a culture or subculture or group survive, so the media can be looked upon as serving a cultural continuity function.

MOBILIZATION

Many mass culture theorists argue, on the other hand, that the media are dysfunctional—that they destroy subcultures and lead to the development of mass societies characterized by alienated, separated individuals who feel powerless and who can be easily manipulated or "mobilized." This theory is a kind of localized version of cultural imperialism theory, except that it is the people who live in a given country, such as the United States, who are assumed to be "brainwashed" or dominated, or whatever term one wishes. If millions of people are watching the same programs on television, so the theory goes, they can, without recognizing what is occurring, be indoctrinated with certain ideologies and beliefs. This theory assumes that everyone is getting the same message or "reading" the texts more or less the same way. Whether this is an accurate description of the situation is very questionable.

A variant of mobilization theory claims that the media are "narcotizing," that they make people passive and apathetic. Individuals must process so much information poured into them by the media, so many demands are placed on their attention, that this "clutter" overloads their ability to cope. Such information overload is theorized to lead to apathy and enervation. However, this theory assumes a lack of selectivity on the part of audience members, and that people pay the same amount of attention to every message they are exposed to. In fact, when people watch television nowadays, for example (assuming they are not using the remote control to create their own mosaic television shows), they are also often doing other things—eat-ing, chatting with others in person or on the telephone, reading newspapers and magazines, making love, and so on. Sometimes they are doing a number of these things at the same time.

A Note on Dysfunctions and Latent Functions

When we talk about functions, we must also keep in mind dysfunctions and latent functions. I have mentioned, in passing, some suggested dysfunctions of mass communication: the creation of mass societies, ideological indoctrination, and bored, apathetic publics. We also must think about the latent functions of mass communication—that is, the unintended, unexpected, often hidden consequences of the media and the texts they carry. Are we, as Neil Postman (1986) has suggested, "amusing ourselves to death"? Are television narratives making young, impressionable children afraid of strong emotional relationships with others? Is advertising selling something besides the products it pitches? This matter of unintended consequences and latent functions is something we always have to keep in mind, because the latent functions of the media may be those that have the most potential to do harm—or perhaps to do good.

How do we balance the good things we get from mass communication with the bad? In the next section I address some of the criticisms that have been leveled against popular culture, the mass media, and mass communication, and then present some of the defenses that have been offered to counter these criticisms.

Some Criticisms of Mass Media and Mass Communication

Over the years, there have been many attacks on mass communication by researchers, clergy, educators, and others—including those who work in the media. Some of the more common criticisms include the following:

- Fragmentation in the mass media leads to and reinforces fragmentation in our lives.

- The mass media encourage escapism.
- The mass media act as narcotics and lead to media addiction.
- The mass media overwhelm individual tastes and lead to cultural homogenization.
- The development of mass communication media leads to passivity and privatism in people and distracts them from more serious matters.
- The mass media debase sexuality; they distort society's view of women and use sexuality to sell products.
- The mass media present a false picture of reality.
- The mass media create stereotypes and give people false views of others and themselves.
- The mass media enhance ethnocentrism.

We must keep in mind that these attacks generally presuppose "strong" effects from the media of mass communication and assume that viewers, listeners, and readers are getting more or less the same messages from given texts. Each of these criticisms is discussed in turn below.

FRAGMENTATION

The criticism that the media lead to fragmentation reverses the actual order of events. Instead of art imitating life (the mimetic theory), the fragmentation hypothesis suggests that life imitates art, more or less, and that chaotic media, full of different kinds of programs and cluttered with advertising appeals, have negative impacts on audiences in general and individuals in particular. There may be something to this idea, but it is likely that those negatively affected are people whose grip on reality is impaired in the first place.

ESCAPISM

There is an element of escapism to the media, but elite art forms such as the novel, the theater, and the opera also contain such an element. In all art forms that employ narrative, the audience members' willing "suspension of disbelief" allows them to empathize with the characters and forget, for a while, their own various problems and obligations. There is also an element of escapism in music, but this suspension is always momentary, and may, in fact, renew our ability to cope with reality.

A considerable amount of the mass media is taken up with news programs, documentaries, and educational programs of one sort or another. This material is not escapist in nature; in fact, it could be argued that it is just the opposite.

ADDICTION

We know that there are addicts of all kinds as far as the media are concerned. Some people watch television 70-80 hours a week, or read several romance novels every day, or see a dozen or so films per week. But these cases are the exceptions. Most people are not addicts, even though they may watch too much television each day, as far as educators and some psychologists are concerned. We also tend to reserve the term *addict* in regard to media use for those who consume the mass media. Would we call a person who reads serious novels for 10 hours a day an addict? We probably would not, because we have been led to believe that great novels enhance our understanding of life and enrich us, whereas the content of the mass media is essentially junk.

CULTURAL HOMOGENIZATION

The notion that the mass media lead to cultural homogenization is at the heart of the mass culture argument. The suggestion is that the mass media must, inevitably, lead to a mass society full of people who have lost their individuality, their private tastes, and their local and regional cultures. I suggest that just the opposite is occurring, and that we are moving toward popular cultural anarchy. There is little evidence in the United States, Western Europe, and other societies that have developed mass communication industries that homogenization is the norm.

PASSIVITY AND PRIVATISM

If you take a medium such as television, there is good reason to argue that the commercials, the most expensive and dominant genre on television, do direct people's attention away from public matters and focus their attention on their private lives and on consumption.

Commercial advertising and other aspects of the media may be responsible for the development of privatism in American society during the 1980s, but we must also remember that privatism was championed by Ronald Reagan and many other politicians, so it is unfair to blame it all on the media.

Commercials also compete with (and are often shown during breaks in) other kinds of programs that have the opposite effects and that people see as more important. And it can be argued that the media make us aware of certain situations that lead us in the opposite direction, and give "oppositional" groups notoriety and a certain kind of legitimacy. So it is not certain that television and the media in general are the main factors behind the privatism that has been so dominant in the United States in recent years. In addition, the Clinton administration has attacked privatism and has emphasized the public sphere; it can be argued that the mass media have helped carry this message.

DEBASEMENT OF SEXUALITY

Feminist critics of mass communication make the important argument that mass media texts tend to debase women and sexuality. Generally speaking, women are underrepresented in mass media texts, the roles they do have are often demeaning, and they are often portrayed as victims of crimes and/or abuse or as sexual objects.

Because the media do play a role in the formation of people's identities, negative representations of women in the media can have negative effects on women and on society in general. Young women, who model their identities to varying degrees on women they see in the media (in books, newspapers, magazines, films, and television shows), are given stereotyped and inappropriate views of what they can expect in life and what their roles will be. Young males also learn absurd notions about what women are like and how to relate to them.

Gaye Tuchman, a sociologist, has written an interesting essay with the provocative title "The Symbolic Annihilation of Women by the Mass Media" (1978) that deals with the image of women in the media. Although the media may not have "strong" effects in every area, there is evidence that they have a significant impact on sex role stereotyping. In the years since Tuchman's essay was published there have been changes, of course, but the situation has not improved dramatically.

FALSE PICTURE OF REALITY

The criticism that the media present a false picture of reality is a generalized version of the criticism regarding portrayals of women. Some critics argue that the media present a false picture not only of women, but of the world in general. If the media are mimetic—that is, if they imitate reality—the reflection they offer is highly distorted, because they focus upon a narrow range of themes and topics (ones that involve sex and violence, for the most part).

Many sociologists and other kinds of researchers have investigated the content of media texts and have collected evidence that the media are, in fact, obsessed with certain subjects and themes—ones that help them attract audiences. In the case of television, George Gerbner and many others have shown that violence is overrepresented; white male professionals are overrepresented and blue-collar, working-class males (white and of color) are underrepresented; and women, the elderly, and the young are underrepresented.

From the political perspective, some media theorists argue that the media help create a **false consciousness** in their audiences that has social and political repercussions. The media generate texts that carry ideological messages even though those who create the text may not consciously insert such messages. That is, the media are, in essence, manipulative. The people who consume the media gain unrealistic ideas about their life possibilities and are given a picture of reality that justifies the status quo—and this, from an ideological perspective, is of use to those who are members of the ruling classes and want to maintain their power and control. The manipulation thesis, I should point out, has generally been discarded by Marxists and critical thinkers, because it can be argued that all media are manipulative, by definition. The important issue for ideological critics is not whether or not the media are manipulative, but who owns and controls the media.

STEREOTYPING

Because many mass media texts are relatively brief, they often have no time to develop realistic and complex characterization; instead, they use **stereotypes** (generally defined as group-held pictures or images of categories of people) to give audiences a sense of why various characters do things—that is, a theory of motivation. Stereotypes of various racial, ethnic, religious, sexual orientation, and occupational groups are common. Stereotypes sometimes have a grain of truth in them, but generally they are distorted representations; clearly, all members of a group are not like some individuals or some members of that group. Usually, stereotyped images are negative and pernicious, but stereotypes are sometimes based on positive traits.

ETHNOCENTRISM

Some critics charge that the mass media encourage ethnocentrism, the feeling that one's own group (e.g., ethnic group or nation) is the only one that does things the "right" way. On a national level, U.S. media tend to send out the message that we Americans are the good guys; we are at the center of the universe, and American needs and desires are paramount. This view can lead to extreme nationalism and to intolerance for other ways of living and the values of other cultures.

Those who make the criticisms discussed above assume that it is the function of the mass media to reflect reality, to give an accurate picture of it. However, works of fiction, even great works of fiction, have never presented an accurate (from a sociological perspective) picture of society. There are many more neurotic, psychotic, obsessed individuals in our great literary works than in society at large.

Maybe we should see the arts as projective (depicting the reality of the artist) rather than as mimetic (reflecting reality as it is—assuming we can know reality). Some Soviet literary and aesthetic theorists argued that all works should be characterized by "social realism" (i.e., that art should be mimetic), but such realism did a great deal of damage to the arts and was discarded as soon as the Communist government lost power.

I now turn to a topic that more or less subsumes many of the hypotheses discussed above: the matter of domination and resistance as it relates to media usage. There are good reasons, many theorists suggest, to argue that individuals and groups are able to use the media for their own purposes and devices.

Emancipatory and Domination Theories of the Media

For a long time, most of the people working with mass communication saw it as a means of dominating individuals and groups, of shaping their behavior, indoctrinating them with ideological messages, and turning them into passive, alienated, brainwashed victims. In an influential book titled *Mass Culture*, which was published in 1957, Bernard Rosenberg uses such terms as *dehumanizing, standardizing, deadening, exploiting, entrapping, vulgarizing, alienating, cretinizing,* and *brutalizing* to describe his view of mass culture's impacts upon audiences. Mass culture, Rosenberg argues, "cretinizes our taste" and "brutalizes our senses while paving the way to totalitarianism"; it feeds us a steady diet of "cultural pap and gruel"; it provides us with "sleazy fiction, trashy films, and bathetic soap operas," which exacerbate unrest in audiences. Contemporary man "is alienated from his past, from his work, from his community, and possibly from himself" (pp. 5-9). Much of Rosenberg's critique is an application of Marxist theory to the media. This analysis was written, we must remember, in 1957, almost 40 years ago. In recent years some Marxists and other theorists have developed a different perspective on things, what might be called an emancipatory theory of media usage.

Resistance: Emancipatory Uses of Mass Communication

Mass communication must be seen as a two-edged sword. If mass communication can be used to control, it can also be used to resist control and domination—for what can be described as emancipatory purposes. Marxist analyses of mass communication generally display a very high level of abstraction. Sweeping indictments are made, and mass culture and popular culture are accused of doing this or that to society—with little attention paid to specific texts and to the ways various subcultures use these texts. Simon Frith points this out in *Sound Effects: Youth, Leisure, and the Politics of Rock 'n' Roll* (1981), where he discusses Theodore W. Adorno's critique:

> Adorno's is the most systematic and the most searing analysis of mass culture and the most challenging for anyone claiming a scrap of value for the products that come churning out of the music industry. His argument . . . is that modern capital is burdened by the problem of overproduction. Markets can only be stimulated by *creating* needs . . . needs which are the result of capital rather than human logic and therefore, inevitably, false. The culture industry is the central agency in contemporary capitalism for the production and satisfaction of false needs. (pp. 44-45)

This argument stems from Marx's notion that capitalism must create false needs in people in order to maintain itself. There is some question as to whether these so-called false needs are invented or are transformations of real needs that people have.

The problem with Adorno's critique and those of his colleagues in the Frankfurt school, argues Frith, is that they are too abstract, too cerebral, and not based on analyzing the texts or the people who use them. As Frith explains: "The actual use of music by pop fans is scarcely examined—passivity is assumed. The supposed effects of pop are, rather, deduced from the nature of the music itself" (p. 45). Mass culture theorists are able to spin out theories to explain the alleged degeneration of modern European culture, compared with what I would describe as nostalgia for an imaginary, traditional European culture where the elite arts dominated and the status of intellectuals was not challenged by others.

When we look at how individuals and groups use pop music and various other products of popular culture, the situation turns out to be a lot more complicated. In many cases, people use popular culture—the texts carried by the mass media, mass culture, or whatever you wish to call it—for their own purposes, often subverting the content of the texts. Consider, for example, the development of rap music and what might be called hip-hop culture in general as a form of resistance by African American and other groups against the values and beliefs of the dominant American culture.

Humor and Resistance: A Case Study

As an important example of resistance, let me offer the matter of humor, which pervades our lives and is found everywhere, from conversations between people to graffiti to stories, books, television programs, and films. Humor can be used to control individuals and groups, by making certain ideas or behaviors the subject of ridicule. Jokes and other forms of humor about members of certain ethnic, religious, occupational, and other groups have this function.

When we laugh at jokes about gays or cartoons about silly middle-class women (e.g., in the *New Yorker*) or nerds (e.g., *The Far Side*) or comic strips about military figures (e.g., *Beetle Bailey*), we are, though we may not be conscious of it, diminishing them, putting ourselves above them, attacking their claims to legitimacy and authority and suggesting that their behavior is absurd and should not be a model for others. Jokes, I should point out, are a common form of humor, but not the only one; there are many other forms of humor that use a variety of techniques to generate laughter.

The matter of humor's relation to control and resistance is the subject of a book edited by Chris Powell and George E. C. Paton titled *Humour in Society: Resistance and Control* (1988), which contains a number of chapters by social scientists on the ways different forms of humor are related to control and resistance. An essay in this book by Powell, "A Phenomenological Analysis of Humour in Society," deals with this matter in some detail. Human communication of all kinds, Powell suggests, can be looked at as having control elements in it. But this makes control so abstract and wide-ranging as to dilute the usefulness of the concept. The term *control* means different things to different people, he adds:

> Radicals are too easily lulled into the belief that "control" refers exclusively to the practices of "the powerful." "Control" in this usage seems

overly deterministic, hierarchical, totalistic and pessimistic. All social activities in all social institutions, all aspects of public and "private" life pull any such successful subordinates materially and ideologically further into the clutches of their oppressors. Conversely, "resistance" refers to the practices of the powerless struggling to release themselves from the yoke of control. (pp. 98-99)

From a radical's viewpoint, control is bad and resistance is good. A conservative would take the opposite position: Control must be maintained and resistance suppressed.

The ultimate means of social control, Powell suggests, involves the way people perceive social reality and our notions about the place of others in the scheme of things, including the way we relate to others who hold beliefs and values of which we do not approve. This leads to a series of negotiations involving our understanding of others, and this is where humor comes in, for it plays a major role in these negotiations.

Powell is somewhat pessimistic about the ability of people to use humor as a means of resistance; he sees power relationships as affecting the ways people respond to jokes in small groups and in society in general. "Humour is a control resource operating both in formal and informal contexts to the advantage of powerful groups and role-players," he writes (p. 100). He cites an American sociologist, Lewis Coser, to the effect that most joking is directed downward (an example of the "superiority" theory of humor).

I would argue that Powell underestimates the power humor has to liberate people from social control and conventions and to help people resist ideological domination. The wonderful jokes that circulated in the Soviet Union and Eastern Europe during the Communist period are a case in point. Let me offer two jokes to show what I mean. The first is a "Radio Erevan" joke. Radio Erevan is the name of an actual radio station located in what was Soviet Armenia. In these jokes, people call Radio Erevan and ask questions.

Caller: Dear Radio Erevan: Would it be possible to establish socialism in the Sahara?

Radio Erevan: Yes. But after the first five-year plan, we would have to import sand.

This joke ridicules the Soviet Communist ideology and its various five-year plans, all of which offered statistics (all faked) showing how well off the Russians and others in Communist countries were.

Many jokes dealt with the shortage of housing in Russia. Here is a classic one on that subject:

Two writers meet. "I've just written a new book," says Ivan.
"Good. What's it about?" asks Igor.
"A young man meets a woman."
"Ah, a novel," says Igor.
"They fall in love."
"Ah, a love story," says Igor.
"They marry and find an apartment."
"Oh! A fairy tale!"

A huge number of jokes were generated under Communism that ridicule Communist ideology, the officials of the Communist governments, and other aspects of life in the Soviet Union and its satellites. All of these are examples of the humor of resistance, and they played a role, I would suggest, in making possible the Soviet Union's transition to a democratic society.

What we find in humor can also be found in many other texts in folklore and the mass media—aspects of texts that can be used for resistance, even in cases where it would seem that the text is championing the status quo. And now, with the development of rap music, values and beliefs of some African Americans and other rappers that subvert basic American values are very popular—with many white, middle-class youth, it turns out. These young people use rap to help separate themselves from parental control and establish and consolidate their own identities, in the same way that rock and roll, punk rock, and other kinds of music have been used in the past.

The controversy over whether mass communication and the media function as instruments of control or resistance leads to a related matter that bears on this issue—the difference between those researchers who focus on the ideological content of the media and mass communication and those who focus on how it works and how it can be made more efficient and functional. In academic circles, this debate is described as being between critical (that is, ideological) and administrative (that is, empirical and functional) kinds of research.

Administrative Versus Critical Research in Mass Communication

To understand the difference between **administrative research** and **critical research,** it is useful to understand something about how social scientists and communication researchers have tended to operate in the United States as opposed to how such researchers have operated in Europe. In the United States we have, generally speaking, employed empirical, data-collecting, number-crunching methodologies, seeking to obtain useful statistics and then manipulating (or "massaging") these statistics to gain important information. The focus has been, until recently (when Marxist and critical techniques have become popular with a number of scholars), on gathering data, which are then used to interpret and explain phenomena. To employ a metaphor, we can say that this perspective works from the bottom up.

In Europe, on the other hand, a more philosophical and ideological perspective has been dominant. Scholars there have tended to deal with mass communication, the media, social problems, and other matters in terms of ideological beliefs and the role elites and the so-called ruling classes play in the scheme of things. Much of this stemmed from Karl Marx and various thinkers who extended, refined, and modified his concepts. This approach, which may be described as working from the top down, uses logic and deduction from a set of principles to make sense of things.

There has been a kind of convergence, and now many European social scientists make use of statistics and empirical methods and many American social scientists make use of philosophical and ideological theories in their work. Thus we now find mixtures of the two approaches, though at the extremes of the continuum of mass communication research there are administrative theorists on one side and critical methodologists on the opposite side.

In the summer of 1983, the *Journal of Communication* published a special issue titled "Ferment in the Field" that dealt with many of the controversies in communication research. A number of the articles in this issue were devoted to the subject of critical versus administrative research. One of the best descriptions of the difference between the two schools of research came in an article by Dallas W. Smythe and Tran Van Dinh (1983), who note:

> By "administrative" researchable problems we mean how to make an organization's actions more efficient, e.g., how best to advertise a brand of toothpaste, how most profitably to innovate word processors and video display terminals within a corporation, etc. By "critical" researchable problems we mean how to reshape or invent institutions to meet the collective needs of the relevant social community through devices such as direct broadcast satellites, terrestrial broadcast stations and networks, and cable TV, or, at a "micro" level, how to conduct psychotherapy and how to study rumors. By "administrative" tools, we refer to applications of a neopositivist, behavioral theory to the end of divining effects on *individuals*. By "critical" tools, we refer to historical, materialist analysis of the contradictory process in the real world. By "administrative" ideology, we mean the linking of administrative-type problems and tools with interpretation of results that supports, or does not seriously disturb, the status quo. By "critical" ideology, we refer to the linking of "critical" researchable problems and critical tools with interpretations that involve radical changes in the established order. (p. 118)

Administrative research in communication, then, broadly speaking, seeks to maintain the status quo and is conducted to help institutions and organizations function more efficiently. Critical research in communication, in contrast, seeks to raise our level of understanding in order to make possible major changes in society that will render it more democratic, more just.

Critical scholars may use statistics and other empirical methods, but their basic purpose is, ultimately, ideological. They are critical of the status quo, of the role dominant elites, and those who work for them, play in the mass communication field and in society in general. They see administrative researchers as "tools" of the dominant groups, who use these researchers and their expertise to maintain the status quo.

TABLE 5.2 Critical and Administrative Perspectives

Critical Perspectives	Administrative Perspectives
ideological	empirical
tied to Marxist theory	tied to statistics, data analysis
focus on change	help maintain status quo
conflict basic	consensus basic
sociopolitical goals	limited goals: improve efficiency, etc.
public concerns	private concerns
receivers of messages	senders of messages
egalitarians	hierarchical elitists, individualists

Critical researchers tend to be what Wildavsky and his colleagues would describe as "egalitarians," who are interested in raising up the "fatalists" and who focus on what is common in people—their needs—rather than on what differentiates them from one another. Administrative researchers, in Wildavsky's typology, work for "competitive individualists" and "elites" and maybe even believe in their principles. Table 5.2 lists some of the differences between the critical and administrative positions.

The debate between critical and administrative communication theorists is important because a researcher's theoretical orientation determines the kinds of problems he or she works on. Critical scholars were, until the past couple of decades, a relatively small minority, but in recent years their numbers have been growing and now they are a major force in mass communication research.

The whole field of mass communication research has been changing over the years, and many of the topics discussed in this book, such as the development of reader-response theories, along with the spread of semiotic, psychoanalytic, and other theories (essentially from Europe), have had major impacts. We now have a discipline called *cultural studies* (combining the study of popular culture and the study of elite culture) that deals, in considerable detail, with mass communication and mass-mediated texts, and scholars doing this kind of work now come from disciplines such as English, humanities, and philosophy, as well as from their traditional homes—sociology, political science, journalism, and communication.

According to some scholars, most of us now live in a new kind of society, what they call a **postmodern** one, and it is to the topic of postmodernism and its influence on the study of mass communication that I now turn.

Postmodernism and Mass Communication

Postmodernism is a confusing term that is used by different people in different ways—but that can be said about most of the concepts addressed in this book. Literally speaking, *postmodern* refers to a period that has moved beyond (*post,* in Latin, means "after") the **modern** period—the era approximately from the turn of the century, which was characterized by certain literary and artistic conventions and was dominated by a number of great artists and writers. As Mike Featherstone (1991) notes:

> The basic features of modernism can be summarized as: aesthetic self-consciousness; a rejection of narrative structure in favour of simultaneity and montage; an exploration of the paradoxical, ambiguous and uncertain open-ended nature of reality; and a rejection of the notion of an integrated personality in favour of an emphasis on the de-structured, de-humanized subject. (p. 7)

Modernism in art and literature is associated with such names as James Joyce, Franz Kafka, Ezra Pound, William Faulkner, T. S. Eliot, Pablo Picasso, Henri Matisse, Igor Stravinsky, and Eugene Ionesco. These artists and musicians and writers are important because they functioned as scouts; their work anticipated and reflected the mindset that people in general adopted in later years.

In the era of postmodernism, the modernist perspective is abandoned for something else. As far as the arts are concerned, the postmodernists broke down the boundaries that existed between the so-called elite arts (opera, ballet, symphonic music, poetry) and the popular arts, popular culture, or mass culture. In addition, the postmodernists erased the boundaries between everyday life and art. They developed art based on mixed styles (as in Michael Graves's famous office building in Portland, Oregon), pastiche, playfulness, repetitiveness, and an ironic stance. Todd Gitlin (1989) describes the differences between modernism and postmodernism as follows:

In modernism, voices, perspectives, and materials were multiple. The unity of the work was assembled from fragments and juxtapositions. Art set out to remake life. Audacious individual style threw off the dead hand of the past. Continuity was disrupted, the individual subject dislocated. High culture quoted from popular culture.

Postmodernism, by contrast, is completely indifferent to the questions of consistency and continuity. It self-consciously splices genres, attitudes, styles. It relishes the blurring or juxtaposition of forms (fiction-non-fiction), stances (straight-ironic), moods (violent-comic), cultural levels (high-low). It disdains originality and fancies copies, repetition, the recombination of hand-me-down scraps. It neither embraces nor criticizes, but beholds the world blankly, with a knowingness that dissolves feeling and commitment into irony. It pulls the rug out from under itself, displaying an acute self-consciousness about the work's constructed nature. It takes pleasure in the play of surfaces, and derides the search for depth as mere nostalgia. (p. 52)

All of this might sound interesting, but what does it have to do with our lives and with mass communication? According to some influential postmodernist theorists, Americans may not recognize it, but they have constructed the most advanced (if that is the right term) postmodernist society there is. Our postmodernism reveals itself in places like Disneyland and Las Vegas, in films like *Star Wars* and television shows like *Miami Vice* and *Moonlighting*, in performers like Laurie Anderson and David Letterman, and in our ubiquitous shopping malls.

Postmodernism is identified by one important literary and cultural theorist, Frederic Jameson (1984), as representing a new stage in the development of capitalism. Jameson is particularly negative about the way postmodernism has erased the boundary that some intellectuals put between elite culture and mass culture. In this respect, he writes:

This is perhaps the most distressing development of all from an academic standpoint, which has traditionally had a vested interest in preserving a realm of high art or elite culture against the surrounding environment of philistinism, of schlock and kitsch, of TV series and *Reader's Digest* culture, and in transmitting difficult and complex skills of reading, listening and seeing to its initiates. (p. 112)

Jameson may generalize too much, for there are many intellectuals and critics who do not think that our standards are eroding, that the mixing of elite culture with popular culture is a tragedy, or that popular culture is destroying elite culture. There are a number of critics, it should be added, who have never accepted the notion that elite culture and popular culture are significantly different.

If the postmodernists are right, there is an aspect of life we call culture, and the distinctions we used to make between high culture and low or mass culture and between elite culture and popular culture are misleading and harmful. This new understanding of culture has tremendous implications for the study of mass communication, for postmodernism suggests that many of the old arguments about mass culture and mass societies are irrelevant. Or, at least, they have been since the 1960s, when the postmodern era began.

As might be expected, there are some scholars and theorists who believe that talk about postmodernism is a lot of nonsense and that we are not in a postmodern era. Others argue that postmodernism is an invention of intellectuals and critics in the arts and humanities who have seen their authority as interpreters of classic works eroded and made more or less irrelevant by the rise in importance of popular culture and the mass media. These critics and intellectuals have sought out a new topic to maintain their claims to status and significance and have "discovered"—or perhaps invented—postmodernism.

It is here that I will leave the debate. If the postmodernist critics are right, American society is a postmodernist one, and mass communication has played an instrumental role in establishing and maintaining this postmodernist society. The average American man and woman may never have heard of postmodernism, but when they go shopping in a mall they are having a postmodern experience. And when they use their remote controls to scan television shows and create their own pastiche of a program, they are functioning as postmodern artists. The postmodern society that we have created has, whether we recognize it or not, a profound impact upon our daily lives.

SUMMARY

We began this chapter with a discussion of Siebert et al.'s (1963) four dominant systems of mass communication: the Soviet Communist system, the libertarian system, the social responsibility system, and the authoritarian system. Next we looked at how mass communication industries are financed and the U.S. system of private ownership. This was followed by an analysis of some of the more important functions of mass communication: surveillance, integration and correlation, entertainment and play, cultural continuity, and mobilization. There was also a brief discussion of the media's latent functions and dysfunctions. Some common criticisms of the mass media were then taken up, including that they lead to fragmentation, escapism, addiction, cultural homogenization, and privatism; they exploit sexuality; and they present a false view of reality. After this came a section on emancipatory and domination theories of the media. The last two topics discussed were administrative versus critical research in mass communication and postmodernism.

Schematically speaking we may view the process of artistic creation as composed of two phases which may be sharply demarcated from each other, may merge into each other, may follow each other in rapid or slow succession, or may be interwoven with each other in various ways. In designating them inspiration and elaboration, we refer to extreme conditions: One type is characterized by the feeling of being driven, the experience of rapture, and the conviction that an outside agent acts through the creator; in the other type, the experience of purposeful organization and the intent to solve a problem predominate. The first has many features in common with regressive processes: impulses and drives, otherwise hidden, emerge. The subjective experience is that of a flow of thought and images driving toward expression. The second has many features in common with what characterizes "work"—dedication and concentration. These extremes and many intermediary modes have repeatedly been described in observation and self-observation. We are aware of the fact that not all artistic creation derives from inspiration—neither all kinds nor one kind wholly. But wherever art reaches a certain level, inspiration is at work.

Ernst Kris, *Psychoanalytic Explorations in Art*, 1964

CHAPTER 6

THE ARTIST

In Chapter 5 we concerned ourselves with America, and with society in general. Now, in this final chapter, we turn to creative artists and consider their role in mass communication and the mass media. The artist is the last of the five focal points—but not the least important, by any means. I point out in this chapter that some kinds of creative artists, such as novelists, create their own texts, whereas others, such as television scriptwriters, generally work in teams. Some art forms, such as film, are extremely collaborative. All creative artists have to be mindful of the powers and limitations of the media they work in and of the tastes and interests of their potential audiences. This leads to discussion of some of the social functions of art, the stereotypes many people have of artists, and the role of intention in the creative arts. This is followed by a discussion of the psychology of creation based on the ideas of Sigmund Freud, the founder of psychoanalytic theory and one of the seminal (and most controversial) thinkers of the 20th century. I conclude the book with a discussion of auteur theory and a case study of Akira Kurosawa, director of *Rashomon*, as an auteur figure.

Artists tend to be the forgotten men and women in the field of mass communication scholarship. Researchers devote a great deal of attention to audiences and to the media, and to the effects of mass-mediated texts on audiences in particular and on society in general. But there has not been a great deal of attention paid, generally speaking, to the people who write the scripts, perform them, direct the performers, and provide the technical expertise necessary to create texts of all kinds—from commercials to situation comedies to sports shows to dramas.

Kinds of Artists

The term **artist** is understood in this book to refer to all those involved with the creation and production of texts that are distributed, spread, broadcast, narrowcast, cablecast, or beamed by satellite through the mass media. In some art forms, a work generally has a single creator; a novel, for instance, is usually written by a lone writer. In the case of a novel, an editor is also usually involved who may or may not have a strong role in shaping the novel, and various production personnel see the novel into print, but the author is the single creator of the text. Poems, novels, plays, and many other written texts usually have a single creative source. All creative artists need to keep their potential audiences in mind, because, for example, it makes no sense to write a novel if nobody is going to read it, and publishing houses are businesses that have to make a profit.

The production of texts for some media, such as television and film, requires the collaboration of many people: teams of writers, directors, producers, technical experts, performers, and so on. Figure 6.1 displays some of the different people involved in the creation of a typical film: performers (actors, actresses), production artists (film editors, composers and musicians, camera operators, costume designers, lighting experts), the writer or writers who create the screenplay, the director (who "shapes" the film and generally is seen as the most important figure in the production team), and the producer, who secures the financing and plays other roles.

Every film, then, is a team effort, although the director is usually seen as the **auteur,** the "author" or person whose artistic vision most directly shapes the film. In film and television (what are sometimes called the photoelectronic media), the performers are just the tip of

Figure 6.1. Film as a Collaborative Art Form

the iceberg, and hidden below them is an army of other kinds of artists and workers whose talents play a major role in the creation and success of a film or television show. Some successful television comedy programs have half a dozen or more writers working together. *Your Show of Shows,* for example, had a large writing staff, and two of the show's stars, Sid Caesar and Imogene Coca, also had a hand in scriptwriting, along with the program's producer.

The Artist as Encoder

Most texts in the media, except for sports shows and improvisational comedy and a few other kinds of shows, involve writers, who, according to the communication theorists discussed in earlier chapters, encode material that is to be decoded by audiences. Writers must have a sense of who makes up their audiences—what those people are like and what they like—if they are to reach those people, to create texts that large numbers of people will like, listen to, read, or watch.

The mass media tend to print and broadcast works that fall within highly formulaic genres, which makes things easier for audiences to understand and makes it possible for writers to keep up with the demand for material. When radio broadcast large numbers of what we now would call action-adventure shows (*The Lone Ranger, The Green Hornet, Superman,* and others), the use of formulas made it easier for writers to generate the huge numbers of scripts that were needed. Fran Striker, who wrote *The Lone Ranger* radio program, is estimated to have written 60,000 words per week in 1939, with the aid of a small team of writers (see Steiner, 1991). He was responsible for more than 150 radio scripts and 365 comic strips. Striker was able to do this because the show was highly formulaic. The formula, as Striker explained it, involved the following:

1. establishing a character
2. giving him a problem he couldn't solve
3. explaining why he couldn't solve it (due to the actions of some villain)
4. informing the Lone Ranger about the situation
5. having the villain plot to kill the Lone Ranger
6. having the Lone Ranger outwit or outfight the villain and solve the situation

The order of events could be shuffled about, and the characters could be changed (in one story a young man, in another an old lady) so that an endless number of scripts could be generated from this formula (see Steiner, 1991).

Romance novels are another highly formulaic genre, with very precise and detailed rules about what can happen in the plots and what the characters must be like: what the heroines look like, how tall the heroes are, the ages of the various characters, and so on.

Writers and Audiences

One problem that sometimes occurs is that there is no fit between the mind-set of the writers and other artists involved in the creation of a text and that of the audience they are trying to reach. We can assume that artists want to reach the largest audiences they can, and that they create texts with a sense of what their audiences are like. But in some cases the artists' aim is faulty, and they do not create texts that appeal to the audiences they are trying to attract (although they may inadvertently reach other segments of the general public).

In other cases, artists produce poorly written and badly produced texts that appeal to very few people. There is not just one big mass of society out there, but individuals and groups and subcultures that all have different perspectives, different levels of education and sophistication, and different values and beliefs. Television writers, for example, tend to be white and to come from middle- and upper-middle-class backgrounds; they may have difficulties in creating texts that will appeal to people of color and to lower-middle-class and working-class people. As Muriel Cantor (1988) has noted, in explaining how she began her research on television producers:

> I was acquainted with several producers, actors and other creators in the television industry. One was an assistant director who later became the on-line producer (in Hawaii) of *Hawaii Five-0*. Another had been executive on-line producer for a number of series during the 1960s including *Dr. Kildare, The Eleventh Hour* and *Bonanza,* and later with his wife worked one year as head writer for the daytime soap opera *General Hospital*. These and others I met and liked had high regard for the art of serious film making, were intelligent, sensitive, literate and had high personal standards for conducting their lives and personal relationships. Consequently I found it difficult to understand how they could produce programs with low-brow content while expressing high-brow artistic and literary values and preferences in their public lives. (pp. xxx-xxxi)

What happens, Cantor's research suggests, is that writers recognize that they are working in a collaborative medium dominated by business interests, and they do they best they can. She quotes one producer who said, "I want to produce art and Filerman [his coproducer] wants to create trash, and together we make television" (p. xxxi).

Many well-written and beautifully produced texts are not successful (that is, they do not attract large enough audiences). As a rule, however, it is the quality of the writing that is the crucial factor in films and television programs. Generally speaking, poorly written texts fail, because they do not have enough entertainment value and because the performers cannot "rescue" such scripts. The main problem the artists face is in creating texts that appeal to many different segments of the population—texts that have both aesthetic quality and broad appeal. This is not easy.

Not All Texts in the Elite Arts Are Masterpieces

Most texts created by artists are mediocre or failures, and this is not limited to the mass media. A very high percentage of what might be described as "serious" novels and plays (that is, "elite" art) are mediocre at best. Artists, whether they are writing and creating texts for elite or popular audiences, never can be sure how good or bad their creations are, or how those creations will be received by the public. And, of course, reception by the public is no true indicator of the value of a text, either.

In addition, a given artist will produce texts of varying quality over the years; some might be really great works and others might be mediocre or failures. Not all novels written by great novelists are successes. Artists and those involved in the creative arts in general lead "high-risk, high-gain, high-failure" lives. In art forms such as the novel, one person is to blame for an artistic failure—the writer. But in collaborative art forms, with huge teams of individuals involved, who is to blame? As Cantor (1988) writes:

> Probably the most important insight I gained from conducting this research is that television entertainment is created by "committees" of people so closely interrelated that it is unclear who actually generate the ideas and who actually create the television productions that finally appear on the air. It should also be noted that production through consensus not only distributes praise when programs are successful but also protects its participants by diluting the blame for failure. (p. xxxv)

There are differences of opinion about who is of central importance in the creation of television shows, but generally speaking it is the producer who is considered the auteur. Many television producers started off as writers, and some write as well as produce their shows. What should be pointed out here is that the medium, television, plays an important role in shaping the generation of scripts and the production of shows. The medium that artists work in influences what they can do. It is to this topic that we now turn.

The Medium Shapes the Message

To see how a particular medium affects artists and their works, let us consider the example of oil painting. In *Ways of Seeing*, John Berger (1977) explains the profound impact that the advent of painting with oils made upon artists and their patrons. Oil painting, Berger tells us,

is more than a technique; it describes an art form—one that has particular qualities. The age of the traditional oil painting, he calculates, existed between 1500 and 1900, and played an important role. He offers an interesting hypothesis:

> A way of seeing the world, which was ultimately determined by new attitudes to property and exchange, found its visual expression in the oil painting, and could not have found it in any other visual art form.
>
> Oil painting did to appearances what capital did to social relations. It reduced everything to the equality of objects. Everything became exchangeable because everything became a commodity. All reality was mechanically measured by its materiality. (pp. 86-87)

The painters of this period fought the same battle that painters, television writers and producers, and other artists fight today: doing hack work that the business interests want versus following one's own creative vision.

On the Social Functions of Art

According to Alan Gowans (1981, pp. 17-18), a historian of art, artists, through their creations, have several social functions:

- They create substitute imagery of "things or ideas whose memory it was desirable for some reason to preserve."
- They use images "to tell stories or record events."
- They beautify artifacts and environments with their works.
- They create works that persuade people of some values, ideas, beliefs, or the like.

Gowans adds a fifth function to the list, but it is not a social function, per se:

- They express themselves artistically in carrying out the four social functions, without regard (at times) for their audiences.

This fifth function marks a turning point in our understanding of what artists do. At one time, all art had social functions, and no one asked, What is art? or What is an artist? When the focus on artistic expression became dominant, in what we now would call the elite arts, the first four functions of art were taken up by the popular or commercial arts and the artists who worked in these areas. The major part of Gowans's book *Learning to See* is concerned with showing how these functions are manifested in the arts, elite as well as popular, through an examination of the work of a number of creative artists in all mass media—from cartoons and comic strips to soap operas and advertisements.

New Technologies and New Media

Artists in the photoelectronic media now have immense resources at their command—using new technologies, they can do incredible things with images and sound—but they always are restrained by the limitations of their media and their audiences. A television screen is still a relatively small area, and artists working in video and television have to consider the problems the small screen poses for them: their need for close-ups to show detail, their reliance on the z-axis for action shots, and so on. They must also consider the taste level of their projected audience. (There is a philosophical problem of interest here. If a tree falls in a forest but there is nobody around to hear it fall, does it make a sound? Philosophers dispute this matter. Let me ask a related question: If a television show airs but nobody watches it, does it make a sound? The answer is, Yes, but not for long.)

In the background, except for those artists who have had great success and are financially independent as a result, is the problem artists face of making a living, of satisfying decision makers on the business side of things—the people who decide what shows to back and the advertising agency people who decide whether or not to buy advertising time on a given show based on their assessment of what size and kind of audience it might attract.

The medium, then, plays an important role in shaping the artist's work. In the print media, writers of novels, for example, can take chances, because they don't need huge numbers of readers for their publishers to make a profit (and they can make money from tie-ins, such as sales to filmmakers). But in television, where enormous audiences are needed to justify the costs involved in producing programs, it is very difficult to challenge audiences and succeed, though some shows have done so. Films, which often cost $30-40 million to make, are even more problematic.

There is nothing intrinsic in the medium of television that prevents writers and artists from doing good or even great work; it is the economic imperatives in the medium that cause most of the problems. Given the difficulties inherent in our system of financing television, and the fact that radio and television are businesses as well as something else, it is remarkable that so much good work is done. The same applies to films. The development of interactive media, computer technology, virtual reality, and more suggests that there will soon be new opportunities for creative individuals to pursue their work in what might be described as hybrid or even new media.

The Irony of the Artist's Image

In the public mind, ironically, the image of the artist derives from 19th-century **romanticism,** a literary and artistic movement that involved specific notions about creativity. Artists were seen as geniuses who must be allowed to live their lives as they desired and who could not be expected to conform to social norms. As César Graña (1967) writes:

> Genius was unleashed as an all-powerful, radical, and unequalled event, a gift of nature which must be allowed to take its course no matter how disruptive to common perceptions. It was not only the right of the intelligence to be respected, but also the duty of genius to tear up norms, to shatter the confines of rules and to permit a whole new world of reality, uniquely perceived, conceived, and expressed, to emerge out of its oceanic depths. . . . Artistic and literary creation became something formidable, awesome, surrounded by an aura of trance and revelation. (p. 52)

This belief led to bohemianism and the notion that artists and writers (and creative people of all sorts) were more or less required to live unconventional lives.

Grana details a number of other aspects of romanticism: the ideal of self-expression, which must be free; the need for "cosmic self-assertion"; a sense of the hostility of the business world and society toward the artist and creative personality; world-weariness; and disdain for "the horror of daily life." These ideas have led to a stereotype of the creative artist as bohemian, a stereotype that television and film writers have used often in their portrayals of artists.

In actuality, Grana (1967) suggests, bohemians tend to be people of "excitable imaginations and modest talent, a combination which disables them for an ordinary existence and forces them, as a consolation, to a life of dedicated unconventionality" (p. 72). This perspective enabled bohemians to feel important and to live lives that were self-absorbed and self-centered—offering them the best of two worlds.

Writing for the Mass Media

The romantic, bohemian picture of the writer is about as far removed from the way most writers for the mass media live as can be imagined. In television, most shows are written by teams, and writers face enormous pressure to come up with scripts on a regular basis. As they work, these writers must consider, among other things, the natures of the audiences they are writing for, the producers they are working for, and the censors at the networks, who have the power to modify scripts.

What our brief look at the romantic movement of the 19th century shows is that our modern image of the artist stems from an earlier period and tends to be somewhat absurd. It also shows that the tension between artistic and commercial interests was felt even then, and, in truth, has always been felt. There is always a tension between the imagination of the artist and the bank account and taste level of the producer (or, in earlier days, the patron).

It is useful to recall here our discussion of reception theory and the notion that readers of books and texts of all sorts play an important role in the scheme of things. The romantic idea that all the creativity resides in the artist has been attacked, and a good measure of creativity is now attributed to the members of the audience who help "realize" the text. What we have here is a democratization of the idea of creativity: It is no longer the sole possession of the artist; it is now found in audiences as well.

There is good reason to suggest that creativity is found in all people and is not limited to artists and to works that we define as art. Every night, most humans dream for several hours, and those dreams can be seen as narratives reflecting our creativity. Young children tend to be extremely creative, until the educational system and other social forces drive this creativity out of most of them. And, if reception theorists are correct, every text we read and see and hear demands creativity on our part. So there is much more creativity manifested in our daily lives than we tend to imagine.

The Problem of Intention

Some literary critics have argued that in looking at texts we should not concern ourselves with the intentions of the texts' creators; doing so is what they call the **intentional fallacy**. They suggest that what counts is not the intention of the artist but the text itself. We should not interpret the meaning of a text or evaluate the success of a text on the basis of an author's intention.

There is a certain amount of sense to this notion. Many a young writer intends to write the great American novel, but succeeds only in writing a piece of second-rate work. Further, writers may think they know what their works mean, but psychoanalytic theory and literary theory often suggest that they do not. We must assume that artists do not understand the full significance of what they are doing, even if they think they do.

A great deal of the work that goes on in universities is devoted to interpreting and understanding what artists do and various aspects of the creative process. In art departments, literature departments, humanities departments, film and media departments, language departments, and so on, scholars spend their lives trying to understand what artists do, how they work, and what their works mean. If intention were the only significant thing, artists could tell us—they could write little notes about what their paintings and plays and films mean, and there would be nothing much for professors and critics to do.

René Wellek and Austin Warren (1977) discuss the matter of intention:

> The whole idea that the "intention" of the author is the proper subject of literary history seems . . . quite mistaken. The meaning of a work of art is not exhausted by, or even equivalent to, its intention. As a system of values it leads an independent life. The total meaning of a work cannot be defined merely in terms of its meaning for the author and his contemporaries. It is rather the result of a process of accretion, i.e., the history of its criticism by its many readers in many ages. (p. 42)

These authors point out that contemporary readers of ancient texts cannot read them the way the ancients did—people today have different sensibilities.

We must assume, then, that an artist's intention, what the artist thinks he or she is doing, is not terribly significant. But that does not mean the artist's intention has no significance. After all, we must be aware that Woody Allen is filming a comedy when he creates *Sleeper* or that Shakespeare is writing a comedy when he writes *Twelfth Night*. And we should be aware of Woody Allen's and Shakespeare's intentions when we see these works.

Of course, many a comedy writer fails to write a funny work, and thus we have television shows and films that are meant to be funny but are not. The intention of the artist is a factor, then, but it is not the only important element in a text, or even the most important element.

We must trust the text, not the artist—for artists, like everyone else, are quick to make rationalizations and are often confused and self-deceived about themselves and what they are doing. The same applies to critics, which explains why Wellek and Warren (1977) suggest that we have to look at how critics have analyzed a work over the years to gain a sense of what the work is about, recognizing that we are always developing new critical strategies.

The Psychology of Creation: A Freudian Perspective

Why some people become artists and develop the creative aspects of their personalities is a mystery. When we think of the mass media, we know that there are huge amounts of money to be made, so the financial rewards play a role, no doubt. But there are other ways of earning large salaries and making a great deal of money that are much less risky; relatively few people are able to earn a living writing scripts for television shows and films.

In 1908, Sigmund Freud wrote "The Relation of the Poet to Day-Dreaming," an article that offers an interesting explanation of how creative people "come by their material." He suggests that writers (and by implication we can understand all creative artists) are very similar to children at play. According to Freud (1908/1963), the writer

> creates a world of fantasy which he takes very seriously; that is, he invests it with a great deal of affect, while separating it sharply from reality. Language has preserved this relationship between children's play and poetic creation. It designates certain kinds of imaginative creation, concerned with tangible objects and capable of representation, as "plays"; the people who present them are called "players." (p. 35)

There is, then, a strong element of play in both creative artists and performing artists, the so-called players.

As we grow up, Freud continues, we stop playing (the way we did when we were children) and appear to give up the pleasure we

Despite the candor of many distinguished scientists and artists in telling of their work, and despite what we have been able to learn in more general terms about creativity, there is still a great deal that we do not know about it. But this much is clear. The problems, insights, ideas, and forms which come to the artist and to the scientist seem to come as often from the unconscious as the conscious mind, from wide, eclectic, and unorganized reading, observing, or experiencing, from musing, browsing, and dreaming, from buried experiences, as from anything immediately and consciously in view. They come, as Arthur Koestler has shown us in several of his extraordinary works, as often from the "left-handed" processes of feeling and intuition as from the "right-handed" channels of logic, empirical directness, and reason.

Robert Nisbet, *Sociology as an Art Form*, 1976, p. 19

experienced from this play. But we never really give anything up; rather, we exchange one thing for another, and so we find a substitute for our play fantasies in **daydreams** and ultimately in creative works—either by others or those we fashion ourselves.

In this article, Freud actually deals with what we now would call popular culture. He says he will not focus his attention on classics, works highly esteemed by critics, but instead, will

choose the less pretentious writers of romances, novels and stories, who are read all the same by the widest circle of men and women. There is one very marked characteristic in all the productions of these writers which must strike us all: they all have a hero who is the centre of interest, for whom the author tries to win our sympathy by every possible means, and whom he places under the protection of a special providence. If at the end of one chapter the hero is left unconscious and bleeding from severe wounds, I am sure to find him at the beginning of the next being carefully tended and on the way to recovery. (pp. 39-40)

The hero of such works, Freud suggests, is "His Majesty the Ego, the hero of all day-dreams and all novels." In stories, as in daydreams, the good people are those who help the ego fulfill its role as hero; the bad ones are its rivals.

In many creative productions, Freud adds, the original daydream that generated the story is greatly disguised, but ultimately the creative production can be traced back to some strong experience, usually had in childhood, that generated a wish that eventually is fulfilled in the creative work. In an earlier work, *Dreams and Their Relation to the Unconscious*, Freud had suggested that dreams are tied to wish fulfillment. Now, he suggests that creative works are also connected to repressed wishes that more or less generate them, though in highly elaborated and disguised versions. We have emotional responses to works, in part, because we are stimulated by them to enjoy our own daydreams without a sense of shame or guilt.

Freud recognized that understanding how creative artists get their inspiration and their ideas is a problem; in his essay "Dostoevsky and Parricide" (written in 1928) he writes, "Before the problem of the creative artist analysis must, alas, lay down its arms." (This essay on Dostoevsky is a fascinating study of one particular writer; those interested in the creative process will find it worth consulting.)

The main point is that we still do not know a great deal about the creative process, though we generally can recognize people who are first-rate creative and performing artists. (We do not always recognize them in their lifetimes, however, or appreciate their greatness when we do recognize them.) Often, we reward them with a great deal of esteem, money, or both. When it comes to film directors, we sometimes do not recognize talent immediately; we often have to wait until directors do a number of films before we appreciate their talents and understand what is distinctive about their work. It is to that subject I now turn.

Auteur Theory

When we call a film director an auteur, we are making reference to what is distinctive and original in his or her body of work.

The virtual worlds within MUD [multiuser domain or multiuser dimension] systems have many of the social attributes of physical places and many of the usual social mechanisms apply. Users treat the worlds depicted as if they were real. However, it is not the technological interface that sustains the willingness of users to treat this simulated environment as if it were real. Rather, it is the degree to which MUDs act not only as a tool for the expression of each user's imagination but mediate between the user's imagination and the communication to others of what he or she has imagined. Cyberspace—the realm of electronic impulses and high-speed data highways—may be figured as a technological construct, but virtual reality is a construct within the mind of a human being. Within this construct a representation of a person can be manipulated within a representation of a real or imagined environment, both of which can be manifested through the use of various technologies, including computers. Virtual worlds exist not in the technology used to represent them, not purely in the mind of the user, but in the relationship between internal mental constructs and technologically generated representations of these constructs. The illusion of reality lies not in the machinery itself but in the user's willingness to treat the manifestations of his or her imaginings as if they were real.

Elizabeth Reid, "Virtual Worlds," 1995, pp. 165-166

According to auteur theory, directors impose their personalities, their aesthetic sensibilities, their values and beliefs, on every aspect of their films. Before we can determine a particular director's style, view of life, preoccupations, recurring themes, and so on, we have to be able to look at a number of his or her films. Directors are given "authorship" in films because they are, in principle at least, ultimately responsible for the script, the casting, the shooting, the editing, and every other aspect of the production.

It is important to recognize that a director's style and motifs are not always apparent. As Geoffrey Nowell-Smith writes:

> The defining characteristics of an author's work are not necessarily those which are most readily apparent. The purpose of criticism thus becomes to uncover behind the superficial contrasts of subject and treatment a hard core of basic and often recondite motifs. The pattern formed by these motifs . . . is what gives an author's work its particular structure, both defining it internally and distinguishing one body of work from another. (quoted in Wollen, 1972, p. 80)

Wollen (1972) offers, as an example of auteur criticism, an analysis of the work of Howard Hawks, all of whose films "exhibit the same thematic preoccupations, the same recurring motifs and incidents, the same visual style and tempo" (p. 81).

Wollen quotes the filmmaker Jean Renoir, who said that directors spend their whole lives making one film in more or less infinite variation, and auteur critics have to reconstruct this film and analyze its structure. In a sense, this notion is very close to Freud's concept of "repetition compulsion," which describes the need certain neurotics have to repeat certain behaviors over and over again to escape from anxiety. In the case of the auteur, this repetition compulsion is separated from its neurotic base and manifests itself in a body of works that dwell upon certain unconscious preoccupations of the auteur.

A single film can be seen as a figure against the ground of a director's body of films. As Wollen suggests: "It is through the force of his preoccupations that an unconscious, unintended meaning can be decoded in the film, usually to the surprise of the individual involved. The film is not a communication, but an artifact which is unconsciously structured in a certain way" (pp. 167-168). That is, directors are not completely aware of what they are doing, any more than writers or artists are. Much of what happens when an audience views a film or television show involves a kind of hidden communication between the unconscious of the creator of the text and the unconscious of each of the individuals who constitute the audience.

Directors think they know what they are doing when they direct films or television dramas (or whatever) and we who watch these texts think we know what we are getting out of them, but, in reality, the situation is much more complicated than that. We may say, adopting a functional perspective, that we watch *Northern Exposure* because we want to be amused, but why does that program (or any program) amuse us?

Kurosawa as Auteur

This brings us back to Akira Kurosawa and *Rashomon*. Kurosawa, one of the great directors of the modern cinema, has a considerable body of work. *Rashomon*, which appeared in 1950, was, in fact, his eleventh film; he has directed more than a dozen films since *Rashomon*, including such works as *Ikiru*, *The Seven Samurai*, and *Throne of Blood*.

A number of the themes and preoccupations found in Kurosawa's work are of interest here. In his essay "*Rashomon* and Kurosawa," Donald Richie (1969) addresses some of these matters. In his discussion of the differing stories of the characters in *Rashomon*, he writes: "In all of Kurosawa's pictures there is this preoccupation with the conflict between illusion (the reactions of the five) and reality (the fact of the rape and murder). To do something is to realize that it is far different from what one had thought" (p. 225). Another important concern found in Kurosawa's work is his preoccupation with time. As Richie (1969) explains:

> Kurosawa's preoccupation with time (*the* preoccupation for any serious director) began with *Rashomon*. There are two kinds of time which concern him—and any other director. One is ostensible time—the time the story takes. The other is a certain kind of psychological time, the time that each sequence, and that each shot within this sequence takes. (p. 231)

It is Kurosawa's concern with time that leads him to spend almost as much time in the cutting room, editing his films, as he does shooting them. There are 407 separate shots in *Rashomon* (with another 12 used for titles)—more than twice as many as in the average film—and some of these shots are quite long. This means that Kurosawa used many more shots for some scenes than is usual, which is how he created the effects he wanted.

Another commentator on Kurosawa, Dennis DeNitto (1985), suggests that Kurosawa's films all contain a tension between and an alternation of "rigorous control and explosive vigor"; he also points out Kurosawa's use of "striking visual effects" (pp. 175, 176). The famous scenes in *Rashomon* of the woodcutter walking through the forest and of the rape, characterized by Richie as "rhapsodic impressionism," are examples of these remarkable visual effects. DeNitto mentions yet another important aspect of Kurosawa's work:

> What makes the director's films so impressive, however, is that his technical skills are in the service of an unswerving commitment to humanistic concerns. Most of his works with contemporary settings are protests against social injustices. Attaining a degree of goodness in a selfish society, battling for dignity and justice against human indifference, and preserving individuality in an age of conformity are recurrent themes. (p. 176)

This brief discussion of Kurosawa as an auteur illustrates how we can analyze a given film director's work by looking at its technical and stylistic characteristics and at the important social themes that recur in that work. Although it is more difficult to analyze the work of television producers, it is possible to consider the social and political themes that inform their work; Norman Lear, for example, has produced a number of programs that have a definite perspective. Thus, although we may not be able to analyze the work of television producers in the same way we can look at the work of film directors, we still can assess some producers' bodies of work.

We can also use auteur theory to analyze the work of artists in other media, such as writers of comic books, comic strip artists, makers of animated cartoons, songwriters, and writers of popular novels. For some reason, most mass communication theorists have neglected the artist/creative personality (and aesthetic considerations, as well); this impoverishes their work and unnecessarily limits the field of investigation. It is my hope that this chapter functions as a step toward correcting this deficiency.

SUMMARY

This chapter began with a discussion of the different kinds of artists and creative personalities found in the mass media, distinguishing between those that involve individual creators and those that involve collaboration. This was followed by a discussion of the problems artists face as encoders of material that may not be decoded by audiences as the artists thought they would be. Next came an analysis of the relation between artists and the media they work in; the medium may not "be" the message, but it shapes the message in varying ways. We then examined the image of the artist and its connection to 19th-century romanticism and the "cult of the genius." After this came discussion of an aesthetic problem—the question of the artist's intentions and the role of these intentions in how works should be interpreted. This led to a related matter: the psychology of creation and, in particular, Freud's notion that creativity is connected to infantile wishes that were blocked and are later fulfilled in creative activity. The chapter concluded with a discussion of auteur theory in general and an examination of the work of Akira Kurosawa in particular.

APPENDIX

COMBINATIONS: QUESTIONS FOR DISCUSSION AND RESEARCH

We have examined, in some depth, the five focal points that are central to understanding the process of mass communication: the work of art (the text), the audience, the medium, America (society), and the artist. Now I would like to offer a number of suggestions for discussion and research that involve various linkings or combinations of these focal points. These suggestions are offered in the form of questions that might serve as directions for investigation and discussion.

The field of mass communication theory is one in which there are many controversies, which, as I have suggested, is a sign of vitality and life. Wilbur Schramm, one of the founding fathers of the field of communication studies, has described it as a crossroads where many pass through, but few tarry (cited in McAnany, 1991, p. 312). That is, much of the work that is done in mass communication is done by people who are sociologists, psychologists, political scientists, economists, and so on, who become interested in communication and analyze it from the perspectives of their own disciplines. Each of these disciplines has different notions about how one investigates the world, and there are disputes within each field on this matter as well. Until relatively recently, there were no Ph.D. programs in communication. Thus it is understandable why there is so much "ferment" in the field, given that the people who do research in it come from so many different disciplines and have so many different methodological approaches. Most communication departments, even now, are made up of scholars with different disciplinary identities, though the graduate schools of communication are graduating more and more scholars with Ph.D.s in communication per se.

With this in mind, let us consider some of the questions about mass communication that have been raised in this book, as well as others that are deserving of attention.

Art and Artist

1. Is the intention of the artist a significant concern in the analysis of a communication text? If intention is not important, what is important?
2. How does one text by an artist relate to that artist's other work?
3. How does a given text relate to other texts by other artists? How does one limit the notion of *intertextuality*, or can one limit it in any way? Is using a formula an example of intertextuality?
4. In collaborative art forms, who is the *auteur*? How do you justify your choice?
5. How do an artist's age, sex, race, religion, socioeconomic class, geographic region, and general social situation affect his or her work?

Art and Audience

1. What is the relation between the audience and the text? Is there a difference between the "lowest common denominator" and the "largest common denominator"?
2. Is it possible that certain texts "create" their audiences? If so, give examples.
3. Is there a connection between the formulaic nature of certain texts and their audiences? If so, show the connection and give examples.
4. What uses do audiences make of texts and what gratifications do they get from them? Cite specific examples by analyzing a text.
5. Is there a difference between a *use* and a *gratification*?
6. How is it that a particular text can appeal to so many different subcultures in a society? Is there something like "national character" or something else that explains this?

7. Why is it that texts (especially films and television shows) made in America for Americans also appeal to people in other cultures with different values and belief systems?

Art and Medium

1. How does the medium affect the text? Answer this by examining a specific text and showing how the possibilities and limitations in the medium have shaped the text.
2. What role does the ownership of the medium play in the creation of texts? Consider here texts in music, film, television, and the comics as well as newspapers (and print and electronic journalism, in particular).
3. Why is it that heroes and heroines move from medium to medium? Consider such figures as Superman, Batman, Orphan Annie, Li'l Abner, and the characters in *Peanuts.*

Art and America

1. How does a particular text relate to American society, culture, and character? What aspects of society does it emphasize and what aspects does it neglect?
2. How are various groups portrayed by the media? Consider, for example, women, Jews, African Americans, old people, working-class people, the disabled, Arabs, and young children. If these groups are stereotyped, what are the stereotypes? How do stereotypes work? Why are stereotypes used?
3. Does a text essentially reflect the values in the society in which it is found, or does it affect those values? Is there so much violence in American media because we are a violent society, and the texts mirror this violence? Or do these violent texts exacerbate the problem of violence?
4. Is there a vicious cycle relative to violence and the media? Do the media reflect violence and overemphasize it, which then leads to more violence in the society, which the media then reflects and again overemphasizes, leading to a spiral of violence?

Audience and Media

1. How do the attributes of a medium affect its potential audience?
2. Do certain media, irrespective of the texts found in them, tend to attract certain audiences? Is the "medium the message" for these audiences?

3. What role does the economic system play in the development of media?

4. Will the new technologies "democratize" the media and empower audiences, or will we end up with "57 channels and nothing on"?

5. Even if we have 500 cable channels, given that there are only a limited number of genres, will an audience's choices be significantly enhanced?

6. Does the mainstream culture depicted in most of our films and television programs influence the various American subcultures and lead to the homogenization of American society? Do American films and television shows impose our culture on people in other societies?

Audience and America

1. What is the relation that exists between an audience and the society in which the audience is found? Can we say that the larger the audience, the more representative it is?

2. Are audiences "unified," or are they assemblages of people with different demographics: ages, sexes, races, religions, and so on? Is there such a thing as *mass culture*?

3. The theory that there are four political cultures in democratic societies suggests that there are four different media audiences in these societies. Do you think this is the case? What is going on if a hierarchical elitist watches an egalitarian television show? Is it possible that members of all the political cultures can like the same text? If so, use a specific text as an example, to show how this might work.

Audience and Artist

1. How does the potential audience affect the artist? Give specific examples, citing particular texts.

2. Are there differences between the ways artists working in the elite arts and those working in the popular arts relate to their potential audiences? If so, explain the differences.

3. Can artists create their own audiences? New audiences? Justify your answer with examples relating to the work of specific artists and their texts.

4. How do you explain the phenomenon of taste? Why do people like particular artists—actors, actresses, singers, musicians, directors, playwrights?

5. Why are some artists successful in one medium (such as television) and not successful in a different medium (such as film)? Cite specific artists and their case histories.

6. If you could be any kind of artist you wish, what would you be? Explain the rationale for your answer, citing the benefits and negative aspects involved.

Media and Artist

1. How does a given medium affect the work of artists working in that medium? Cite specific examples.
2. Take each of the mass media and consider what aspects can be exploited by artists and what limitations each medium imposes on artists.
3. Which medium do you think allows the greatest possibilities for personal expression and creative achievement? How would you rank the media in this respect? If you could work in any medium, which one would you choose?
4. Do artists who work in media that require collaboration lose something? That is, is creativity intrinsically an individual matter?

General Questions

1. Does the framework of the five focal points (the artist, the work of art, the medium, the audience, and America/society) make it easier for you to understand the field of mass communication, or is it a procrustean bed, forcing various issues into a questionable set of categories? Justify your answer.
2. Can you think of a different way of organizing a book on mass communication that makes more sense? What is it? What advantages does it have over the focal points perspective?
3. Do you think there will ever be a period when there will be no "ferment" in the field of mass communication theory? If so, how will it happen? If not, why not?
4. What criteria do you use in evaluating the truthfulness, validity, and usefulness of a concept? Is it a matter of whether you are familiar with it? Whether it makes sense to you? Whether it explains things well? Just because you think some idea, concept, or theory is ridiculous, does that mean it really is ridiculous? How do you separate your opinion from truthfulness and correctness? On what bases do you hold your opinions?
5. How have you been affected by the process of mass communication and the mass media that are its instruments? Can you think of anything you have done because you were influenced by commercials, characters in texts, songs you have listened to, or some other mass-mediated text?

GLOSSARY

Aberrant decoding: The decoding or interpretation of texts by audiences in ways that differ from the ways the creators of the texts expect them to be decoded. According to semiotician Umberto Eco (1972), aberrant decoding is the rule, rather than the exception, when it comes to the mass media.

Administrative research: Research that focuses on ways of making communication by organizations and other entities more efficient and more effective. Compare with critical research, which has more interest in social justice and related considerations.

Aesthetics: When applied to the media, aesthetics involves how technical matters such as lighting, sound, music, kinds of shots and camera work, editing, and related matters in texts affect the ways members of audiences react.

Agenda-setting theory: The theory that institutions of mass communication determine not what we think, but what we think about. They set the agenda for our decision making and thus influence our social and political lives.

Archetypes: Images found in dreams, myths, works of art, and religions all over the world (see Jung, 1968). Archetypes are not transmitted by culture but are passed on, somehow, genetically, in a collective unconscious. They reveal themselves in our dreams and works of art. One of the most important archetypes is the hero.

Artist: In the context of this volume, anyone involved in the creation or performance of a media text.

Attitude: A relatively enduring state of mind in a person about some phenomenon or aspect of experience. Attitudes generally are either positive or negative, have direction, and involve thoughts, feelings, and behaviors.

Audience: In the context of this volume, a collection of individuals who receive a media text—watch a television program, listen to a radio program, attend a film or some other kind of artistic performance, and so on. Members of an audience may be together in one room or scattered; in the case of television, each may be watching on his or her own set.

Auteur: French word meaning "author," used to point out who is the most significant artist, whose vision dominates, in collective art forms such as film and television. Auteur critics look for hidden themes and stylistic traits in the collected works of film directors.

Broadcast: Made available over wide areas through radio or television signals. Broadcasting is one way of distributing television and radio texts; other ways include cablecasting and satellite transmission.

Class: A group of people or things that have something in common; in this context, social class or, more literally, socioeconomic class—based on income and lifestyle—is of interest.

Codes: Systems of symbols, letters, words, sounds, and so on that generate meaning. Language, for example, is a code. It uses combinations of letters that we call words to mean certain things. The relation between the word and the thing the word stands for is arbitrary, based on convention. In some cases, the term *code* is used to describe hidden meanings and disguised communications.

Cognitive dissonance: The psychological conflict that results within a person when he or she holds clashing beliefs or when his or her actions and beliefs are opposed to each other. In general, people wish to avoid exposure to ideas that challenge those they hold, because entertaining new ideas can create inner conflict and other disagreeable feelings.

Collective representations: Broadly speaking, texts that reflect the beliefs and ideals of groups and other collectivities. Durkheim (1967) uses this concept in addressing the fact that people are both individuals, pursuing their own aims, and social animals, guided by the groups and societies in which they find themselves.

Communication: A process that involves the transmission of messages from senders to receivers. We often make a distinction between communication that uses language (verbal communication) and communication through facial expressions, body language, gesture, and the like (nonverbal communication).

Communications: The messages communicated during the process of communication, described above.

Concept: A general idea or notion that explains or aids in the understanding of some phenomenon or phenomena.

Content analysis: A nonintrusive methodology in which the researcher examines particular elements in a text or collection of texts to quantify them and use them for statistical analysis.

Convergent selective conditions: Decisions we make about relatively minor matters, ones that are not tied to deeply held beliefs, which are described as social controls in Stephenson's (1967/1988) play theory.

Critical research: Approaches to media that are essentially ideological, that focus on the social dimensions of the mass media and the way they are used by organizations and others allegedly to maintain the status quo rather than to enhance equality. Compare with administrative research.

Cultivation theory: The theory that television dominates the symbolic environment of its audiences and gives people false views of what reality is like. That is, television cultivates or reinforces certain beliefs in its viewers, such as the notion that society is permeated by violence.

Cultural homogenization: The destruction of cultures (such as Third World and certain regional cultures) other than the dominant culture, leading to cultural sameness and standardization.

Cultural imperialism or **media imperialism:** The alleged domination of Third World cultures through the transmission of certain values and beliefs via the flow of media products (such as songs, films, and television programs) and popular culture from the United States and a few Western European capitalist countries.

Culture: The specific ideas, arts, customary beliefs, ways of living, behavior patterns, institutions, and values of a group, transmitted from generation to generation. When applied to the arts, the term *culture* is generally used in reference to "elite" kinds of artworks, such as operas, poetry, classical music, and serious novels.

Daydreams: Dreamlike musings and fantasies that people have while they are awake.

Defense mechanisms: The methods used by the ego to defend itself against pressures from the id, or impulsive elements in the psyche, and superego elements such as conscience and guilt. Some of the more common defense mechanisms are repression (barring unconscious instinctual wishes, memories, and so on from consciousness), regression (returning to earlier stages in one's development), ambivalence (a simultaneous feeling of love and hate toward some person or thing), and rationalization (offering excuses to justify one's actions).

Demographics: Statistical characteristics of people, including race, religion, gender, social class, ethnicity, occupation, place of residence, and age.

Deviance: Difference from the norm, whether in values and beliefs or in actions.

Dysfunctional: Contributing to the breakdown or destabilization of an entity.

Ego: The executant of the id and a mediator between the id and the superego. The ego is involved with the perception of reality and the adaptation to reality.

Emotive function: The function of expression of feelings. This is one of the functions of messages, according to Jakobson (1988); others are referential and poetic.

Ethical criticism: Criticism that is concerned with moral aspects of texts and the texts' possible impacts.

Ethnocentrism: The belief that the ideas, customs, values, way of life, and so on of one's own group (ethnic group, nation, or other body) are better than those of other groups.

Expressive theories of art: Theories based in the notion that the principal function of art is to express the feelings, beliefs, and emotions of the creators of works of art.

False consciousness: In Marxist thought, the mistaken ideas that people have about their class, status, and economic possibilities. These ideas help maintain the status quo and are of great use to the ruling class, which wants to avoid changes in the social structure. According to Marx, the ideas of the ruling class are always the ruling ideas in society.

Feminist criticism: Criticism that focuses on the roles of women and how women are portrayed in texts of all kinds. Feminist critics argue that women are typically depicted as sexual objects or in other stereotyped ways in texts, and that this has negative societal effects for both men and women.

Flashback: A scene in a narrative text that depicts action that took place at an earlier time; used to explain motivation or to provide other kinds of information.

Focal points: In the context of this volume, the five general topics or subject areas used to organize the discussion of mass communication: the work of art or text, the artist, the audience, America or society, and the media.

Formula: In the context of this volume, a set pattern of characters and actions used in a narrative text and with which audiences are familiar. Genre texts, such as detective stories, westerns, science fiction adventures, and romances, are highly formulaic.

Functional: Helping to maintain a system. A functional institution contributes to the maintenance of society.

Functional alternative: Something that functions to take the place of something else. For example, professional football can be seen as a functional alternative to religion.

Gatekeepers: Those with the power to determine who or what gets to pass through a certain point. In the context of this volume, gatekeepers include the editors who determine which stories are used in newspapers and on television and radio news programs. In a broader sense, gatekeepers determine which programs and films we see, what songs we hear, and so on.

Gender: The sexual category of an individual—masculine or feminine—and the behavioral traits connected with each category.

Genre: A type of text characterized by a particular style, such as soap opera, news show, sports program, horror show, or detective story. In French, *genre* means "kind" or "class." (For in-depth discussion of genre texts, see Berger, 1992.)

Hypodermic needle theory: The theory, generally discredited now, that holds that all members of an audience "read" a text the same way and get the same things out of it. The metaphor of a hypodermic needle is a reference to how media are assumed to be injecting all audience members with the same message.

Hypothesis: An assumption that something is true for the purposes of discussion or argument or further investigation. In a sense, a hypothesis is a guess or supposition that is made as a basis from which to explain some phenomenon.

Id: The element of the psyche that is the representative of a person's drives, according to Freud's theory of the psyche (his "structural hypothesis"). Freud (1933) calls the id "a chaos, a cauldron of seething excitement." It also is the source of energy, but it lacks direction, and so the ego must harness and control it. In popular thought, the id is connected with impulse, with "I want it all now" kind of behavior.

Ideology: A logically coherent, integrated explanation of social, economic, and political matters that helps establish the goals and direct the actions of some group or political entity. People act (and vote or do not vote) on the basis of their ideologies, even those who have never articulated or given any thought to them.

Image: In the context of this volume, "a collection of signs and symbols—what we find when we look at a photograph, a film still, a shot of a television screen, a print advertisement, or just about anything" (Berger, 1989, p. 38). An image may be a mental or a physical representation. Images can have powerful emotional effects on people, and some images have historical significance. (For in-depth discussion of image, see Adatto, 1993; Messaris, 1994.)

Intentional fallacy: The idea that it is an error to consider the intention of the artist an important element in the analysis of that artist's work. This has been the subject of considerable debate; some critics believe that we *should* consider an artist's intention in analyzing his or her texts, to some degree at least.

Latent functions: Hidden, unrecognized, and unintended functions of some activity, entity, or institution. These are contrasted by social scientists with manifest functions, which are recognized and intended.

Lifestyle: The way people live, including the decisions they make about how to decorate their homes (and where they are located), the kinds of cars they drive, the styles of clothes they wear, the kinds of foods they eat and the restaurants they go to, where they go for vacations, and so on.

Limited effects (of media): Minor effects of media on society. Some mass communication theorists argue that the influence of the mass media is relatively small in the larger scheme of things. They cite research that shows, for example, that effects from media do not tend to be long lasting.

Manifest functions: Obvious and intended functions of some activity, entity, or institution. These are contrasted by social scientists with latent functions, which are hidden and unintended.

Mass: In the context of this volume, a large number of people who form the audience for some communication. There is considerable disagreement about how to understand the mass of people who are reached by mass communication. Some theorists believe the mass is made up of individuals who are heterogeneous, do not know one another, are alienated, and do not have a leader. Others attack these notions as not based on fact or evidence; they assert that such theories concerning the mass are incorrect.

Mass communication: The transfer of messages, information, texts, and the like from a sender of some kind to a large number of people, a mass audience. This transfer is done through the technologies of the mass media—newspapers, magazines, television programs, films, records, computer networks, CD-ROM, and so on. The sender often is a person in some large media organization, the messages are public, and the audience tends to be large and varied.

Mass media: Technically, the instruments by which mass communication is achieved. In common parlance, the media such as radio, television, print, records, and film that carry texts and can be used to communicate to large numbers of people.

Medium: In the context of this volume, *medium* refers to a communication medium—a means of delivering messages, information, and texts to audiences. There are different ways of classifying media, one of the most common of which is to divide them into print (newspapers, magazines, books, billboards), electronic (radio, television, computers, CD-ROM), and photographic (photographs, films, videos).

Metaphor: A figure of speech that conveys meaning by analogy. It is important to realize that metaphors are not confined to poetry and literary works; according to some linguists, the fundamental way we make sense of things and find meaning in the world is through metaphors. A simile is a weaker form of metaphor that explicitly uses either *like* or *as* in making an analogy.

Metonymy: A figure of speech that conveys information by using the name of one thing to describe another with which it is associated (for example, using the name Rolls Royce to convey that something is expensive or high quality). Along with metaphor, one of the most important ways people communicate information to one another is through metonymy, although we tend not to be aware of how much we use association to get our ideas across.

Mimetic theories of art: Theories, dating from Aristotle's time, based in the notion that art imitates reality.

Model: In the context of this volume, an abstract representation that shows how some phenomenon functions. Theories are typically expressed in language, but models tend to be represented graphically or through statistics or mathematics. McQuail and Windahl (1993) define a model as "a consciously simplified description in graphic form of a piece of reality. A model seeks to show the main elements of any structure or process and the relationships between these elements" (p. 2).

Modern: Falling within the period approximately from the beginning of the 20th century to the 1960s. Modernist artists rejected narrative structure for simultaneity and montage and explored the paradoxical nature of reality. Important modernists include T. S. Eliot, Franz Kafka, James Joyce, Pablo Picasso, Henri Matisse, and Eugene Ionesco.

Narrowcast: Disseminate a media text narrowly, by focusing on particular discrete groups. This contrasts with broadcasting, which tries to reach as many people as possible.

Nonfunctional: Neither functional nor dysfunctional. Something that is nonfunctional plays no role in the maintenance or breakdown of the entity in which it is found.

Nonverbal communication: Communication that does not involve words; carried out through body language, facial expressions, styles of dress, hairstyles, and so on.

Objective theories of art: Theories based in the notion that art functions to project reality (that of the artist), like a lamp, as opposed to reflecting reality, like a mirror.

Opinion leader: A person whose opinions influence those of others. Opinion leaders play an important role in the two-step flow theory of communication.

Phallic symbol: An object that resembles the penis, either in shape or function. Symbolism is a defense mechanism of the ego that permits hidden or repressed sexual or aggressive thoughts to be expressed in disguised form (for further discussion of this topic, see Freud, 1965).

Phallocentric: Dominated by the masculine point of view. Some critics assert that the ultimate source of this domination, that which shapes our institutions and cultures, is the male phallus. In this theory, a link is made between male sexuality and male power. (More detailed discussion of this concept is found in Berger, 1995.)

Poetic function: The function of expression through poetic language. According to Jakobson (1988), one of the functions of messages is the use of such literary devices as metaphor and metonymy. Messages also have emotive functions and referential functions.

Political cultures: Cultures comprising people who are similar in terms of their political values and beliefs and in relation to the group boundaries and rules and prescriptions they observe. Wildavsky (1989) asserts that all democratic societies have four political cultures and need these cultures to balance off one another. He calls the members of these four cultures individualists, hierarchical elitists, egalitarians, and fatalists. For an example of how Wildavsky's theories can be applied to mass media and popular culture, see Berger (1990).

Popular: Literally, "of the people" (from the Latin *popularis*). This term can be defined in many ways, but for purposes of this volume, it generally is used in the sense of appealing to large numbers of people.

Popular culture: The culture of the people, usually understood to include certain kinds of texts that appeal to large numbers of people. Mass communication theorists often identify (or confuse) *popular* with *mass*, and suggest that if something is popular, it must be of poor quality, appealing to the mythical "lowest common denominator." Popular culture is generally held to be the opposite of "elite" culture, which includes arts that require a certain level of sophistication and refinement to appreciate, such as ballet, opera, poetry, and classical music. Many critics now question this popular culture/elite culture polarity.

Postmodern: Falling within the period after the modern era, or from approximately the 1960s to the present. According to a leading theorist on the subject, Jean-François Lyotard (1984), postmodernism is characterized by "incredulity toward metanarratives" (p. xxiv). In other words, the old philosophical belief systems that had helped people order their lives and societies are no longer accepted. This has led to a period in which, more or less, anything goes.

Power: The ability to implement one's wishes as far as policy in some entity is concerned. In the discussion of texts, *power* is also used to describe their ability to have emotional impacts upon people—readers, viewers, or listeners.

Pragmatic theories of art: Theories based in the notion that art must do something, must have certain consequences that are held to be desirable. Thus art should teach, or indoctrinate, or perform some other function.

Psychoanalytic theory: A theory based on the notion that the human psyche includes an element Freud calls the "unconscious" that is ordinarily inaccessible to us (unlike consciousness and the preconscious) and that continually shapes and affects our mental functioning and behavior. Imagine an iceberg: The tip of the iceberg, showing above the water, represents consciousness; the part of the iceberg that is visible just below the surface of the water represents the preconscious; and the rest of the iceberg (most of it), which we cannot see (but we know is there), represents the unconscious. We cannot access this area of our psyches because of repression.

Psychographics: A marketing term (combining the words *psychological* and *demographics*) to describe the psychological characteristics of groups of people.

Public: A group of people, a community. Terms such as *public arts* and *public communication* are sometimes substituted for *popular culture* and *mass communication* to avoid the negative connotations of the words *mass* and *popular*. *Public* is also used in opposition to *private*, as in public acts—those meant to be known to the community—contrasted with private acts—those not meant to be known to others.

Rationalization: In Freudian thought, a rationalization is a defense mechanism of the ego that creates a justification for some action (or for inaction when an action is expected).

Reader-response theory or **reception theory:** The theory that readers (who include those who read books, watch television programs, go to films, and listen to texts on the radio) play an important role in the realization of texts. Texts, then, function as sites for the creation of meaning by readers, and different readers will interpret a given text differently.

Referential function: The function of the expression of relationships between people and/or things. According to Jakobson (1988), the referential function of messages is to help speakers relate to their surroundings. He contrasts this with emotive and poetic functions of speech.

Relativism: In philosophical thought, the belief that truth is relative and not
absolute; there are no objective standards. In ethical thought, relativism
suggests there are no moral or ethical absolutes. Thus different cultures
have different ways of living and practices that are as valid as those of
any other culture. That is, morality and ethical behavior are relative to
particular groups and cannot be generalized to include all human
beings. This contrasts with the notion that there are ethical absolutes
or universals that can and should be applied to everyone.

Role: A socialized way of behaving that is appropriate to a particular
situation. A person generally plays many roles with different people
during a given day: parent, student, worker, and so on.

Romanticism: A 19th-century movement in artistic and literary endeavor in
which emotion, feeling, freedom from social restraints, and similar
notions were stressed.

Sapir-Whorf hypothesis: The hypothesis that language is not something transparent that merely conveys information from one person to another but
something that affects the ways people think and act. According to this
hypothesis, language is not like a windowpane but more like a prism.

Secondary modeling system: The system beyond that of language, our first
modeling system (Lotman, 1977), through which we use language to
create art.

Selective attention: Attention paid only to what we choose. We have a
tendency to avoid messages that conflict with our beliefs and values
(see *cognitive dissonance*, above).

Semiotics: Literally, the science of signs (from the Greek *semion*, meaning
"sign"). A sign is anything that can be used to stand for anything else.
According to C. S. Peirce, one of the founders of the science, a sign "is
something which stands to somebody for something in some respect
or capacity" (quoted in Zeman, 1977, p. 24). (See Berger, 1984, for
discussion of many important concepts in semiotics and how they can
be applied to popular culture.)

Serial texts: Texts that continue over long periods of time. Examples include
comic strips and soap operas and other television narratives that are
on for extended periods of time. Serial texts pose the problem for critics
of deciding what to consider when analyzing the text—the whole of the
series or individual episodes?

Shadow: In Jungian thought, the dark side of the psyche, which we attempt to keep hidden. The shadow contains repressed and unfavorable aspects of our personalities as well as normal instincts and creative impulses. Thus in all of us there is a continual battle between shadow aspects of our personalities and our egos, which also contain some negative features.

Social class: A term used by sociologists to refer to people who occupy or have a similar place, by virtue of matters such as education, occupation, taste, and lifestyle in the class structure. In America it has been suggested we have, according to W. Lloyd Warner, six classes: upper-upper, lower-upper, upper-middle, lower-middle, upper-lower, and lower-lower, each with distinctive traits and behavior patterns. Social class does not always correlate with income and socioeconomic class. A garbage collector may have a higher salary than a clergyman, but that does not translate automatically into higher social class.

Social controls: Ideas, beliefs, values, and mores of a society that shape people's beliefs and behaviors.

Socialization: The process by which societies teach individuals how to behave: what rules to obey, roles to assume, and values to hold. Socialization has traditionally been a function of the family, educators, clergy, and peers, but the mass media are serving as a socializing force to a considerable degree nowadays, with consequences that are not always positive.

Socioeconomic class: A group categorized according to income and related social status and lifestyle. In Marxist thought, history is, in essence, a record of socioeconomic class conflict between the ruling class and the working class.

Status: Whereas class refers to something that people have in common, status deals with one's relative rank in some stratified entity. There are two kinds of status: *achieved* status, which we gain through our own efforts, and *ascribed*, or awarded status, which we are given due to birth (into royalty, for example), race, religion, gender, age, and so on.

Stereotypes: Commonly held, simplistic, and often inaccurate group-held portraits of categories of people. Stereotypes can be positive, negative, or mixed, but generally they are negative in nature. Stereotyping always involves gross overgeneralizations.

Subculture: A subgroup within the dominant culture that differs in religion, ethnicity, sexual orientation, beliefs, values, behaviors, lifestyles, or in some other way from the dominant culture. Any complex society is likely to have a considerable number of subcultures.

Superego: The agency in the psyche that is related to conscience and morality. According to Freud, the superego is involved with processes such as approval and disapproval of wishes on the basis or whether or not they are moral, critical self-observation, and sense of guilt over wrong-doing. The functions of the superego are largely unconscious, and are opposed to the id element in the psyche. Mediating between the two, and trying to balance them, is the ego.

Text: In the context of this volume, any work of art in any medium. The term *text* is used by critics as a convenience, to avoid the need to specify particular kinds of works.

Theory: A systematic and logical attempt, expressed in language, to explain and predict phenomena. Theories differ from concepts, which define phenomena that are being studied, and from models, which are abstract, usually graphic in nature, and explicit about what is being studied.

Trickster figure: In Jungian thought, a figure who represents the earliest period in the development of the hero. Characteristics of the trickster include mischievousness, physical appetites that dominate behavior, desire for the gratification of primary needs, and actions that are often cynical, cruel, and unfeeling.

Two-step flow theory: The theory that mass communication reaches and affects people in a two-step process: First, the media influence opinion leaders; second, the opinion leaders influence others.

Typology: A classification scheme or system of categories used to make sense of some phenomenon.

Uses and gratifications theory: A sociological theory that audiences use communication media for certain purposes and that they gain certain gratifications from the use of those media. Researchers who subscribe to this theory focus on how audiences use the media, rather than on how the media affect audiences.

Values: Abstract and general beliefs or judgments about what is right and wrong, or good and bad, that have implications for individuals' behavior and for social, cultural, and political entities. From a philosophical point of view, values are the source of several problems. First, how does one determine which values are correct or good and which are wrong or bad? That is, how do we justify our values? Are values objective or subjective? Second, what happens when groups that hold different central values conflict?

Youth culture: A subculture formed by young people around some area of life interest, usually connected with leisure and entertainment, such as rock music or some aspect of computers—games, hacking, and so on. Typically, youth cultures adopt distinctive ways of dressing and develop institutions that cater to their needs. (Frith, 1981, discusses this topic at length.)

SUGGESTED
FURTHER READING

Abelove, H., Barale, M. A., & Halperin, D. (Eds.). (1993). *The lesbian and gay studies reader*. New York: Routledge.

Adorno, T. W. (1967). *Prisms* (S. Weber & S. Weber, Trans.). Cambridge: MIT Press.

Adorno, T. W. (1991). *The culture industry: Selected essays on mass culture*. London: Routledge.

Aitken, S. C., & Zonn, L. E. (1994). *Place, power, situation and spectacle: A geography of film*. Lanham, MD: Rowman & Littlefield.

Armstrong, N. (1987). *Desire and domestic fiction: A political history of the novel*. New York: Oxford University Press.

Aronowitz, S. (1992). *The politics of identity*. New York: Routledge.

Aronowitz, S. (1993). *Dead artists, live theories, and other cultural problems*. New York: Routledge.

Atkin, C., & Wallack, L. (1992). *Mass communication and public health*. Newbury Park, CA: Sage.

Bakhtin, M. (1981). *The dialogic imagination* (M. Holmquist, Ed.; C. Emerson & M. Holmquist, Trans.). Austin: University of Texas Press.

Bakhtin, M. (1984). *Rabelais and his world* (H. Iswolsky, Trans.). Bloomington: Indiana University Press.

Bal, M. (1985). *Narratology: Introduction to the theory of narrative*. Toronto: University of Toronto Press.

Barker, M., & Beezer, A. (1992). *Reading into cultural studies*. London: Routledge.

Barthes, R. (1970). *Writing degree zero and elements of semiology* (A. Lavers & C. Smith, Trans.). Boston: Beacon.

Barthes, R. (1972). *Mythologies* (A. Lavers, Trans.). New York: Hill & Wang.

Barthes, R. (1974). *S/Z* (R. Miller, Trans.). New York: Hill & Wang.

Barthes, R. (1975). *The pleasure of the text* (R. Miller, Trans.). New York: Hill & Wang.

Barthes, R. (1975). *Roland Barthes by Roland Barthes* (R. Howard, Trans.). New York: Hill & Wang.

Barthes, R. (1977). *Empire of signs* (S. Heath, Trans.). New York: Hill & Wang.

Barthes, R. (1978). *A lover's discourse* (R. Howard, Trans.). New York: Hill & Wang.

Barthes, R. (1988). *The semiotic challenge* (R. Howard, Trans.). New York: Hill & Wang.

Bateson, G. (1972). *Steps to an ecology of mind*. New York: Ballantine.

Baudrillard, J. (1983). *Simulations* (P. Foss et al., Trans.). New York: Semiotext(e).

Baudrillard, J. (1994). *Symbolic exchange and death* (I. Grant, Trans.). London: Sage.

Beilharz, P., Robinson, G., & Rundell, J. (1992). *Between totalitarianism and postmodernity: A thesis eleven reader*. Cambridge: MIT Press.

Bennett, T., & Woollacott, J. (1987). *Bond and beyond: The political career of a popular hero*. New York: Methuen.

Berger, A. A. (1973). *The comic-stripped American*. New York: Walker.

Berger, A. A. (1984). *Signs in contemporary culture: An introduction to semiotics*. New York: Annenberg-Longman.

Berger, A. A. (Ed.). (1987). *Visual sociology and semiotics*. Aachen, Germany: Edition Herodot.

Berger, A. A. (1989). *Seeing is believing: An introduction to visual communication*. Mountain View, CA: Mayfield.

Berger, A. A. (Ed.). (1990). *Agitpop: Political culture and communication theory*. New Brunswick, NJ: Transaction.

Berger, A. A. (1991). *Media analysis techniques* (rev. ed.). Newbury Park, CA: Sage.

Berger, A. A. (1993). *An anatomy of humor*. New Brunswick, NJ: Transaction.

Berger, A. A. (1994). *Blind men and elephants: Perspectives on humor*. New Brunswick, NJ: Transaction.

Berger, A. A. (1995). *Cultural criticism: A primer of key concepts*. Thousand Oaks, CA: Sage.

Berman, M. (1982). *All that is solid melts into air: The experience of modernity*. New York: Touchstone.

Bernstein, R. J. (1992). *The new constellation: The ethical-political horizons of modernity/postmodernity*. Cambridge: MIT Press.

Best, S., & Kellner, D. M. (1991). *Postmodern theory: Critical interrogations*. New York: Guilford.

Bettelheim, B. (1976). *The uses of enchantment: The meaning and importance of fairy tales*. New York: Knopf.

Bhabha, H. K. (1993). *The location of culture*. New York: Routledge.

Bird, J., Curtis, B., Putnam, T., & Tickner, L. (Eds.). (1993). *Mapping the futures: Local cultures, global change*. London: Routledge.

Blau, H. (1992). *To all appearances: Ideology and performance*. London: Routledge.

Bogart, L. (1985). *Polls and the awareness of public opinion*. New Brunswick, NJ: Transaction

Bourdieu, P. (1994). *Sociology in question* (R. Nice, Trans.). London: Sage.

Bourdieu, P., & Passeron, J.-C. (1990). *Reproduction in education, society and culture* (2nd ed.). London: Sage.

Bowlby, R. (1993). *Shopping with Freud: Items on consumerism, feminism and psychoanalysis*. London: Routledge.

Bramson, L. (1961). *The political context of sociology*. Princeton, NJ: Princeton University Press.

Branigan, E. (1992). *Narrative comprehension and film*. New York: Routledge.

Brenkman, J. (1993). *Straight, male, modern: A cultural critique of psychoanalysis*. New York: Routledge.

Brenner, C. (1974). *An elementary textbook of psychoanalysis*. Garden City, NY: Anchor.

Brown, M. E. (Ed.). (1990). *Television and women's culture: The politics of the popular*. Newbury Park, CA: Sage.

Brown, M. E. (1994). *Soap opera and women's talk: The pleasure of resistance*. Thousand Oaks, CA: Sage.

Buck-Morss, S. (1989). *The dialectics of seeing: Walter Benjamin and the arcades project*. Minneapolis: University of Minnesota Press.

Butler, J. (1993). *Bodies that matter*. New York: Routledge.

Cantor, M. G. (1988). *The Hollywood TV producer: His work and his audience*. New Brunswick, NJ: Transaction.

Cantor, M. G., & Cantor, J. M. (1991). *Prime-time television: Content and control*. Newbury Park, CA: Sage.

Carey, J. W. (Ed.). (1988). *Media, myths, and narratives: Television and the press*. Newbury Park, CA: Sage.

Clark, K., & Holmquist, M. (1984). *Mikhail Bakhtin*. Cambridge, MA: Harvard University Press.

Clarke, J. (1992). *New times and old enemies: Essays on cultural studies and America*. London: Routledge.

Collins, J., Radner, H., & Collins, A. P. (Eds.). (1992). *Film theory goes to the movies: Cultural analysis of contemporary film*. New York: Routledge.

Collins, R., Curran, J., Garnham, N., Scannell, P., Schlesinger, P., & Sparks, C. (Eds.). (1986). *Media, culture and society: A critical reader*. London: Sage.

Cottom, D. (1989). *Text and culture: The politics of interpretation*. Minneapolis: University of Minnesota Press.

Coward, R., & Ellis, J. (1977). *Language and materialism: Developments in semiology and the theory of the subject*. London: Routledge & Kegan Paul.

Crane, D. (1992). *The production of culture: Media and the urban arts*. Newbury Park, CA: Sage.

Creed, B. (1993). *The monstrous-feminine: Film, feminism, psychoanalysis*. London: Routledge.

Creedon, P. J. (1993). *Women in mass communication* (2nd ed.). Newbury Park, CA: Sage.

Crimp, D. (Ed.). (1988). *AIDS: Cultural analysis/cultural activism*. Cambridge: MIT Press.

Crook, S., Pakulski, J., & Waters, M. (Eds.). (1992). *Postmodernization: Change in advanced society*. London: Sage.

Cross, G. (1993). *Time and money: The making of a consumer culture*. London: Routledge.

Culler, J. (1975). *Structuralist poetics: Structuralism, linguistics, and the study of literature*. Ithaca, NY: Cornell University Press.

Culler, J. (1977). *Ferdinand de Saussure*. New York: Penguin.

Culler, J. (1981). *The pursuit of signs*. Ithaca, NY: Cornell University Press.

Culler, J. (1982). *On deconstruction*. Ithaca, NY: Cornell University Press.

Danesi, M. (1994). *Messages and meanings: An introduction to semiotics.* Toronto: Canadian Scholars' Press.

Danesi, M., & Santeramo, D. (Eds.). (1992). *Introducing semiotics: An anthology of readings.* Toronto: Canadian Scholars' Press.

Davis, R. C., & Schleifer, R. (1991). *Criticism and culture.* London: Longman.

de Certeau, M. (1984). *The practice of everyday life* (S. Rendall, Trans.). Berkeley: University of California Press.

de Certeau, M. (1986). *Heterologies: Discourse on the other* (B. Massumi, Trans.). Minneapolis: University of Minnesota Press.

DeFleur, M. D., & Ball-Rokeach, S. (1982). *Theories of mass communication* (4th ed.). New York: Longman.

DeFleur, M. L., & Larsen, O. N. (1987). *The flow of information: An experiment in mass communication.* New Brunswick, NJ: Transaction.

De Lauretis, T. (1984). *Alice doesn't: Feminism, semiotics, cinema.* Bloomington: Indiana University Press.

De Lauretis, T. (1987). *Technologies of gender: Essays on theory, film, and fiction.* Bloomington: Indiana University Press.

Denney, R. (1989). *The astonished muse.* New Brunswick, NJ: Transaction.

Denzin, N. K. (1991). *Images of postmodern society: Social theory and contemporary cinema.* London: Sage.

Derrida, J. (1967). *Of grammatology* (G. C. Spivak, Trans.). Baltimore: Johns Hopkins University Press.

Derrida, J. (1981). *Positions* (A. Bass, Trans.). Chicago: University of Chicago Press.

Doane, M. A. (1987). *The desire to desire: The woman's film of the 1940s.* Bloomington: Indiana University Press.

Doane, M. A. (1991). *Femmes fatales.* New York: Routledge.

Donald, J., & Hall, S. (Eds.). (1985). *Politics and ideology.* Bristol, PA: Taylor & Francis.

Douglas, M. (1975). *Implicit meanings: Essays in anthropology.* London: Routledge & Kegan Paul.

Douglas, M. (1992). *Risk and blame: Essays in cultural theory.* London: Routledge.

Duncan, H. D. (1985). *Communication and the social order.* New Brunswick, NJ: Transaction.

Dundes, A. (1987). *Cracking jokes: Studies in sick humor cycles and stereotypes.* Berkeley, CA: Ten Speed.

Durkheim, E. (1967). *The elementary forms of religious life.* New York: Free Press.

Dworkin, D. L., & Roman, L. G. (1992). *Views beyond the border country: Raymond Williams and cultural politics.* New York: Routledge.

Dyer, R. (1993). *The matter of images: Essays on representations.* London: Routledge.

Eagleton, T. (1976). *Marxism and literary criticism.* Berkeley: University of California Press.

Eagleton, T. (1983). *Literary theory: An introduction.* Minneapolis: University of Minnesota Press.

Easthope, A. (1991). *Literary into cultural studies.* London: Routledge.

Eco, U. (1976). *A theory of semiotics.* Bloomington: Indiana University Press.

Eco, U. (1984). *The role of the reader.* Bloomington: Indiana University Press.

Ehrmann, J. (Ed.). (1970). *Structuralism.* Garden City, NY: Anchor.

Elam, K. (1980). *The semiotics of theatre and drama.* London: Methuen.

Ettema, J. S., & Whitney, D. C. (Eds.). (1994). *Audiencemaking: How the media create the audience.* Thousand Oaks, CA: Sage.

Ewen, S. (1976). *Captains of consciousness*. New York: McGraw-Hill.

Ewen, S., & Ewen, E. (1992). *Channels of desire: Mass images and the shaping of American consciousness* (rev. ed.). Minneapolis: University of Minnesota Press.

Featherstone, M. (Ed.). (1988). Postmodernism [Special issue]. *Theory, Culture & Society, 5*(2-3).

Featherstone, M. (1991). *Consumer culture and postmodernism*. London: Sage.

Ferguson, R., Gever, M., Minh-ha, T. T., & West, C. (Eds.). (1990). *Out there: Marginalization and contemporary cultures*. Cambridge: MIT Press.

Fiske, J. (1989). *Reading the popular*. Winchester, MA: Unwin Hyman.

Fiske, J. (1989). *Understanding popular culture*. Winchester, MA: Unwin Hyman.

Fiske, J., & Hartley, J. (1978). *Reading television*. London: Methuen.

Fjellman, S. M. (1992). *Vinyl leaves: Walt Disney World and America*. Boulder, CO: Westview.

Franklin, S., Lury, C., & Stacey, J. (1992). *Off-centre: Feminism and cultural studies*. London: Routledge.

Freud, S. (1960). *A general introduction to psychoanalysis* (J. Riviere, Trans.). New York: Washington Square.

Freud, S. (1963). *Jokes and their relation to the unconscious* (J. Strachey, Trans.). New York: W. W. Norton.

Freud, S. (1965). *The interpretation of dreams* (J. Strachey, Trans.). New York: Avon.

Frith, S. (1981). *Sound effects: Youth, leisure, and the politics of rock 'n' roll*. New York: Pantheon.

Fry, W. F. (1968). *Sweet madness: A study of humor*. Palo Alto, CA: Pacific.

Frye, N. (1957). *Anatomy of criticism*. Princeton, NJ: Princeton University Press.

Gandelman, C. (1991). *Reading pictures, viewing texts*. Bloomington: Indiana University Press.

Garber, M. (1993). *Vested interests: Cross-dressing and cultural anxiety*. New York: Harper Perennial.

Garber, M., Matlock, J., & Walkowitz, R. (Eds.). (1993). *Media spectacles*. New York: Routledge.

Garber, M., Parmar, P., & Greyson, J. (Eds.). (1993). *Queer looks: Perspectives on lesbian and gay film and video*. New York: Routledge.

Gitlin, T. (1985). *Inside prime time*. New York: Pantheon.

Glasgow Media Group. (1976). *Bad news*. London: Routledge & Kegan Paul.

Glasgow Media Group. (1980). *More bad news*. London: Routledge & Kegan Paul.

Goldstein, A., Jacob, M. J., Rorimer, A., & Singerman, H. (1989). *A forest of signs: Art in the crisis of representation*. Cambridge: MIT Press.

Greenblatt, S. J. (1992). *Learning to curse: Essays in early modern culture*. New York: Routledge.

Gronbeck, B., Farrell, T. J., & Soukup, P. A. (Eds.). (1991). *Media, consciousness, and culture: Explorations of Walter Ong's thought*. Newbury Park, CA: Sage.

Grossberg, L. (1992). *We gotta get out of this place: Popular conservatism and postmodern culture*. New York: Routledge.

Grossberg, L., Nelson, C., & Treichler, P. A. (Eds.). (1992). *Cultural studies*. New York: Routledge.

Grotjahn, M. (1966). *Beyond laughter: Humor and the subconscious*. New York: McGraw-Hill.

Guiraud, P. (1975). *Semiology*. London: Routledge & Kegan Paul.

Gumbrecht, H. U. (1992). *Making sense in life and literature* (G. Burns, Trans.). Minneapolis: University of Minnesota Press.

Habermas, J. (1979). *Communication and the evolution of society* (T. McCarthy, Trans.). Boston: Beacon.

Habermas, J. (1987). *The philosophical discourse on modernity: Twelve lectures* (F. G. Lawrence, Trans.). Minneapolis: University of Minnesota Press.

Habermas, J. (1989). *The new conservatism: Cultural criticism and the historians' debate* (S. W. Nicholsen, Trans.). Minneapolis: University of Minnesota Press.

Hall, S. (1988). *The hard road to renewal*. London: Verso.

Hall, S. (1991). *New times: The changing face of politics in the 1990s*. London: Routledge.

Hall, S., & Jefferson, T. (Eds.). (1990). *Resistance through rituals: Youth subcultures in postwar Britain*. London: Routledge.

Hall, S., & Whannel, P. (1967). *The popular arts: A critical guide to the mass media*. Boston: Beacon.

Hartley, J. (1992). *The politics of pictures: The creation of the public in the age of popular media*. London: Routledge.

Hartley, J. (1992). *Tele-ology: Studies in television*. London: Routledge.

Haug, W. F. (1971). *Critique of commodity aesthetics: Appearance, sexuality, and advertising in capitalist society* (R. Bock, Trans.). Minneapolis: University of Minnesota Press.

Haug, W. F. (1987). *Commodity aesthetics, ideology, and culture*. New York: International General.

Hoggart, R. (1992). *The uses of literacy*. New Brunswick, NJ: Transaction.

Holland, N. (1975). *Five readers reading*. New Haven, CT: Yale University Press.

Hoover, S. M. (1988). *Mass media religion: The social sources of the electronic church*. Newbury Park, CA: Sage.

Hutcheon, L. (1989). *The politics of postmodernism*. London: Routledge.

Jacobs, N. (Ed.). (1992). *Mass media in modern society*. New Brunswick, NJ: Transaction.

Jakobson, R. (1985). *Verbal art, verbal sign, verbal time* (K. Pomorska & S. Rudy, Eds.). Minneapolis: University of Minnesota Press.

Jameson, F. (1971). *Marxism and form: Twentieth century dialectical theories of literature*. Princeton, NJ: Princeton University Press.

Jameson, F. (1981). *The political unconscious*. Ithaca, NY: Cornell University Press.

Jameson, F. (1992). *The geopolitical aesthetic: Cinema and space in the world system*. Bloomington: Indiana University Press.

Jameson, F. (1992). *Signatures of the visible*. New York: Routledge.

Jauss, H. R. (1982). *Aesthetic experience and literary hermeneutics* (M. Shaw, Trans.). Minneapolis: University of Minnesota Press.

Jauss, H. R. (1982). *Toward an aesthetic of reception* (T. Bahti, Trans.). Minneapolis: University of Minnesota Press.

Jensen, J. (1990). *Redeeming modernity: Contradictions in media criticism*. Newbury Park, CA: Sage.

Jhally, S., & Lewis, J. (1992). *Enlightened racism: The Cosby Show, audiences, and the myth of the American dream*. Boulder, CO: Westview.

Jones, E. (1949). *Hamlet and Oedipus*. New York: W. W. Norton.

Jones, S. G. (1992). *Rock formation: Music, technology, and mass communication*. Newbury Park, CA: Sage.

Jones, S. G. (Ed.). (1995). *CyberSociety: Computer-mediated communication and community*. Thousand Oaks, CA: Sage.

Jowett, G. S., & Linton, J. M. (1989). *Movies as mass communication*. Newbury Park, CA: Sage.

Jowett, G. S., & O'Donnell, V. (1992). *Propaganda and persuasion* (2nd ed.). Newbury Park, CA: Sage.

Jung, C. G. (Ed.). (1968). *Man and his symbols*. New York: Dell.

Kaplan, E. A. (1982). *Motherhood and representation*. London: Routledge.

Kellner, D. (1992). *The Persian Gulf TV war*. Boulder, CO: Westview.

Korzenny, F., & Ting-Toomey, S. (Eds.). (1992). *Mass media effects across cultures*. Newbury Park, CA: Sage.

Lacan, J. (1966). *Écrits: A selection* (A. Sheridan, Trans.). New York: W. W. Norton.

Larsen, N. (1989). *Modernism and hegemony: A materialist critique of aesthetic agencies*. Minneapolis: University of Minnesota Press.

Lavers, A. (1982). *Roland Barthes: Structuralism and after*. Cambridge, MA: Harvard University Press.

Lazere, D. (Ed.). (1987). *American media and mass culture: Left perspectives*. Berkeley: University of California Press.

Lefebvre, H. (1984). *Everyday life in the modern world* (S. Rabinovitch, Trans.). New Brunswick, NJ: Transaction.

Lévi-Strauss, C. (1967). *Structural anthropology*. Garden City, NY: Doubleday.

Levy, M. R., & Gurevitch, M. (Eds.). (1994). *Defining media studies: Reflections on the future of the field*. New York: Oxford University Press.

Lipsitz, G. (1990). *Time passages: Collective memory and American popular culture*. Minneapolis: University of Minnesota Press.

Lotman, J. M. (1976). *Semiotics of cinema*. Ann Arbor: Michigan Slavic Contributions.

Lotman, J. M. (1977). *The structure of the artistic text* (G. Lenhoff & R. Vroon, Trans.). Ann Arbor: Michigan Slavic Contributions.

Lotman, J. M. (1991). *Universe of the mind: A semiotic theory of culture*. Bloomington: Indiana University Press.

Lull, J. (1991). *Popular music and communication*. Newbury Park, CA: Sage.

Lyotard, J.-F. (1984). *The postmodern condition: A report on knowledge*. Minneapolis: University of Minnesota Press.

MacCabe, C. (1985). *Tracking the signifier: Theoretical essays on film, linguistics, and literature*. Minneapolis: University of Minnesota Press.

MacCannell, D., & MacCannell, J. F. (1982). *The time of the sign: A semiotic interpretation of modern culture*. Bloomington: Indiana University Press.

MacDonald, J. F. (1994). *One nation under television*. Chicago: Nelson-Hall.

Mandel, E. (1985). *Delightful murder: A social history of the crime story*. Minneapolis: University of Minnesota Press.

Martín-Barbero, J. (1993). *Communication, culture and hegemony: From the media to mediations*. London: Sage.

Massumi, B. (1992). *A user's guide to capitalism and schizophrenia: Deviations from Deleuze and Guattari*. Cambridge: MIT Press.

Mattelart, A., & Mattelart, M. (1992). *Rethinking media theory* (J. A. Cohen & M. Urquidi, Trans.). Minneapolis: University of Minnesota Press.

McCarthy, T. (1991). *Ideals and illusions: On reconstruction and deconstruction in contemporary critical theory*. Cambridge: MIT Press.

McCue, G., with Bloom, C. (1993). *Dark knights: The new comics in context*. Boulder, CO: Westview.

McLuhan, M. (1965). *Understanding media: The extensions of man*. New York: McGraw-Hill.

McLuhan, M. (1970). *Culture is our business*. New York: McGraw-Hill.

McLuhan, M., & Fiore, Q. (1967). *The medium is the message*. New York: Bantam.

McQuail, D. (1992). *Media performance: Mass communication and the public interest.* Newbury Park, CA: Sage.

McQuail, D. (1994). *Mass communication theory: An introduction* (2nd ed.). London: Sage.

Mellencamp, P. (1990). *Indiscretions: Avant-garde film, video and feminism.* Bloomington: Indiana University Press.

Mellencamp, P. (Ed.). (1990). *Logics of television: Essays in cultural criticism.* Bloomington: Indiana University Press.

Messaris, P. (1994). *Visual literacy: Image, mind and reality.* Boulder, CO: Westview.

Metz, C. (1982). *The imaginary signifier: Psychoanalysis and the cinema* (C. Britton et al., Trans.). Bloomington: Indiana University Press.

Mindess, H. (1971). *Laughter and liberation.* Los Angeles: Nash.

Modleski, T. (1984). *Loving with a vengeance: Mass-produced fantasies for women.* New York: Routledge.

Modleski, T. (Ed.). (1986). *Studies in entertainment: Critical approaches to mass culture.* Bloomington: Indiana University Press.

Modleski, T. (1988). *The women who knew too much: Hitchcock and feminist theory.* New York: Routledge.

Moores, S. (1994). *Interpreting audiences: The ethnography of media consumption.* London: Sage.

Morley, D. (1988). *Family television: Cultural power and domestic leisure.* London: Routledge.

Morley, D. (1993). *Television audiences and cultural studies.* London: Routledge.

Mulvey, L. (1989). *Visual and other pleasures.* Bloomington: Indiana University Press.

Naremore, J., & Brantlinger, P. (Eds.). (1991). *Modernity and mass culture.* Bloomington: Indiana University Press.

Nash, C. (Ed.). (1990). *Narrative in culture.* London: Routledge.

Navarro, D. (Ed.). (1993, Summer). Postmodernism: Center and periphery [Special issue]. *South Atlantic Quarterly.*

Nichols, B. (1981). *Ideology and the image: Social representation in the cinema and other media.* Bloomington: Indiana University Press.

Nichols, B. (1992). *Representing reality: Issues and concepts in documentary.* Bloomington: Indiana University Press.

Penley, C. (1989). *The future of an illusion: Film, feminism, and psychoanalysis.* Minneapolis: University of Minnesota Press.

Phelan, J. (Ed.). (1989). *Reading narrative: Form, ethics, ideology.* Columbus: Ohio State University Press.

Piddington, R. (1963). *The psychology of laughter.* New York: Gamut.

Powell, C., & Paton, G. E. C. (Eds.). (1988). *Humour in society: Resistance and control.* New York: St. Martin's.

Prindle, D. F. (1993). *Risky business: The political economy of Hollywood.* Boulder, CO: Westview.

Propp, V. (1968). *The morphology of the folktale* (2nd ed.). Austin: University of Texas Press. (Original work published 1928)

Propp, V. (1984). *Theory and history of folklore* (A. Y. Martin & R. P. Martin, Trans.). Minneapolis: University of Minnesota Press.

Ramet, S. P. (Ed.). (1993). *Rocking the state: Rock music and politics in Eastern Europe and the Soviet Union.* Boulder, CO: Westview.

Real, M. R. (1989). *Supermedia: A cultural studies approach.* Newbury Park, CA: Sage.

Reinelt, J. G., & Roach, J. R. (Eds.). (1993). *Critical theory and performance*. Ann Arbor: University of Michigan Press.

Richter, M., & Bakken, H. (1992). *The cartoonist's muse: A guide to generating and developing creative ideas*. Chicago: Contemporary Books.

Rouch, I., & Carr, G. F. (Eds.). (1989). *The semiotic bridge: Trends from California*. Berlin: Mouton de Gruyter.

Ryan, M., & Kellner, D. M. (1988). *Camera politica: The politics and ideology of contemporary Hollywood film*. Bloomington: Indiana University Press.

Sabin, R. (1993). *Adult comics: An introduction*. London: Routledge.

Said, E. (1983). *The world, the text, and the critic*. Cambridge, MA: Harvard University Press.

Saint-Martin, F. (1990). *Semiotics of visual language*. Bloomington: Indiana University Press.

Saussure, F. de. (1966). *A course in general linguistics* (W. Baskin, Trans.). New York: McGraw-Hill.

Schechner, R. (1993). *The future of ritual: Writings on culture and performance*. London: Routledge.

Schneider, C., & Wallis, B. (Eds.). (1989). *Global television*. Cambridge: MIT Press.

Schostak, J. (1993). *Dirty marks: The education of self, media and popular culture*. Boulder, CO: Westview.

Schwichtenberg, C. (Ed.). (1992). *The Madonna connection: Representational politics, subcultural identities, and cultural theory*. Boulder, CO: Westview.

Sebeok, T. A. (Ed.). (1977). *A perfusion of signs*. Bloomington: Indiana University Press

Sebeok, T. A. (Ed.). (1978). *Sight, sound, and sense*. Bloomington: Indiana University Press.

Seldes, G. (1994). *The public arts*. New Brunswick, NJ: Transaction.

Shukman, A. (1977). *Literature and semiotics: A study of the writings of Yuri M. Lotman*. Amsterdam: North-Holland.

Silverman, K. (1983). *The subject of semiotics*. New York: Oxford University Press.

Skovman, M. (Ed.). (n.d.). *Media fictions*. Aarhus, Denmark: Aarhus University Press.

Smith, G. (Ed.). (1991). *On Walter Benjamin: Critical essays and recollections*. Cambridge: MIT Press.

Smith, P. (1988). *Discerning the subject*. Minneapolis: University of Minnesota Press.

Spivak, G. C. (1992). *Outside in the teaching machine*. New York: Routledge.

Staake, B. (1991). *The complete book of caricature*. Cincinnati, OH: North Light.

Steidman, S. (1993). *Romantic longings: Love in America 1830-1980*. New York: Routledge.

Stephenson, W. (1988). *The play theory of mass communication*. New Brunswick, NJ: Transaction.

Szondi, P. (1986). *On textual understanding* (H. Mendelsohn, Trans.). Minneapolis: University of Minnesota Press.

Todorov, T. (1975). *The fantastic: A structural approach to a literary genre* (R. Howard, Trans.). Ithaca, NY: Cornell University Press.

Todorov, T. (1981). *Introduction to poetics* (R. Howard, Trans.). Minneapolis: University of Minnesota Press.

Todorov, T. (1984). *Mikhail Bakhtin: The dialogical principle*. Minneapolis: University of Minnesota Press.

Traube, E. G. (1992). *Dreaming identities: Class, gender, and generation in 1980s Hollywood movies*. Boulder, CO: Westview.

Turner, B. S. (1990). *Theories of modernity and postmodernity*. London: Sage.

Van Zoonen, L. (1994). *Feminist media studies*. London: Sage.

Volosinov, V. N. (1987). *Freudianism: A critical sketch* (I. R. Titunik, Trans.). Bloomington: Indiana University Press.

Weibel, K. (1977). *Mirror mirror: Images of women reflected in popular culture.* Garden City, NY: Anchor.

Wernick, A. (1991). *Promotional culture.* London: Sage.

Willemen, P. (1993). *Looks and frictions: Essays in cultural studies and film theory.* Bloomington: Indiana University Press.

Williams, R. (1958). *Culture and society: 1780-1950.* New York: Columbia University Press.

Williams, R. (1976). *Keywords.* New York: Oxford University Press.

Williams, R. (1977). *Marxism and literature.* New York: Oxford University Press.

Williams, R. (1990). *Notes on the underground: An essay on technology, society, and the imagination.* Cambridge: MIT Press.

Williamson, J. (1978). *Decoding advertisements: Ideology and meaning in advertising.* London: Marion Boyars.

Willis, P. (1990). *Common culture: Symbolic work at play in the everyday cultures of the young.* Boulder, CO: Westview.

Wilson, C. C., & Gutiérrez, F. (1985). *Minorities and media: Diversity and the end of mass communication.* Beverly Hills, CA: Sage.

Winick, C. (1994). *Desexualization in American life: The new people.* New Brunswick, NJ: Transaction.

Wollen, P. (1972). *Signs and meaning in the cinema.* Bloomington: Indiana University Press.

Wollen, P. (1993). *Raiding the icebox: Reflections on twentieth-century culture.* Bloomington: Indiana University Press.

Wright, W. (1975). *Sixguns and society: A structural study of the western.* Berkeley: University of California Press.

Zizek, S. (1991). *Looking awry: An introduction to Jacques Lacan through popular culture.* Cambridge: MIT Press.

REFERENCES

Abrams, M. H. (1958). *The mirror and the lamp: Romantic theory and the critical tradition.* New York: W. W. Norton.

Adatto, K. (1993). *Picture perfect: The art and artifice of public image making.* New York: Basic Books.

Bagdikian, B. (1985). The U.S. media: Supermarket or assembly line? *Journal of Communication, 35*(3).

Bagdikian, B. (1988). Concentration of control of the media. In A. A. Berger (Ed.), *Media USA* (pp. 479-488). New York: Longman.

Ball-Rokeach, S., & Cantor, M. G. (1986). Introduction: The media and the social fabric. In S. Ball-Rokeach & M. G. Cantor (Eds.), *Media, audience, and social structure.* Beverly Hills, CA: Sage.

Bauer, R. A. (1964). The obstinate audience: The influence process from the point of view of social communication. *American Psychologist, 19,* 319-328.

Berger, A. A. (1977, May). Fear of feeling: Vicious cycles in videoland and the real world. *Human Behavior.*

Berger, A. A. (1984). *Signs in contemporary culture: An introduction to semiotics.* New York: Annenberg-Longman.

Berger, A. A. (Ed.). (1988). *Media USA.* New York: Longman.

Berger, A. A. (1989). *Seeing is believing: An introduction to visual communication.* Mountain View, CA: Mayfield.

Berger, A. A. (1990). *Agitpop: Political culture and communication theory.* New Brunswick, NJ: Transaction.

Berger, A. A. (1992). *Popular culture genres: Theories and texts.* Newbury Park, CA: Sage.

Berger, A. A. (1995). *Cultural criticism: A primer of key concepts*. Thousand Oaks, CA: Sage.

Berger, J. (1977). *Ways of seeing*. New York: Penguin.

Bernstein, B. (Ed.). (1977). *Class, codes and control*. London: Routledge & Kegan Paul.

Blumer, H. (1936). The moulding of mass behavior through motion pictures. *Publications of the American Sociological Society, 29*, 115-127.

Brewer, J., & Hunter, A. (1989). *Multimethod research: A synthesis of styles*. Newbury Park, CA: Sage.

Butler, J. (1994). *Television: Critical methods and applications*. Belmont, CA: Wadsworth.

Cantor, M. G. (1988). *The Hollywood TV producer: His work and his audience*. New Brunswick, NJ: Transaction.

Cantril, H., with Gaudet, H., & Herzog, H. (1966). *The invasion from Mars: A study in the psychology of panic*. New York: Harper Torchbooks.

Cawelti, J. (1971). *The six-gun mystique*. Bowling Green, OH: Bowling Green University Popular Press.

Davidson, J. (1969). Memory of defeat in Japan. In D. Richie (Ed.), *Rashomon: A film by Akira Kurosawa*. New York: Grove.

Davison, W. P., Boylan, J., & Yu, F. T. C. (1976). *Mass media: Systems and effects*. New York: Praeger

DeNitto, D. (1985). *Film form and feeling*. New York: Harper & Row.

Dorfman, A., & Mattelart, A. (1975). *How to read Donald Duck: Imperialist ideology in the Disney comic*. New York: International General.

Dorfman, A., & Mattelart, A. (1991). *How to read Donald Duck: Imperialist ideology in the Disney comic* (2nd ed.) (D. Kunzle, Trans.). New York: International General.

Durkheim, E. (1967). *The elementary forms of religious life*. New York: Free Press.

Eco, U. (1972). Towards a semiotic inquiry into the television image. *Working Papers in Cultural Studies, 3*.

Eco, U. (1984). *The role of the reader: Explorations in the semiotics of texts*. Bloomington: Indiana University Press.

Elliott, S. (1993, January 7). Determining demographics by what's on the coffee table. *New York Times*.

Erikson, E. (1968). *Identity, youth, and crisis*. New York: W. W. Norton.

Esslin, M. (1982). *The age of television*. San Francisco: W. H. Freeman.

Featherstone, M. (1991). *Consumer culture and postmodernism*. London: Sage.

Freud, S. (1933). *New introductory lectures on psychoanalysis* (J. Strachey, Trans.). New York: W. W. Norton.

Freud, S. (1963). The relation of the poet to day-dreaming. In S. Freud, *Character and culture: Psychoanalysis applied to anthropology, mythology, folklore, literature, and culture in general* (P. Rieff, Ed.). New York: Collier. (Original work published 1908)

Freud, S. (1965). *The interpretation of dreams* (J. Strachey, Trans.). New York: Avon.

Friedman, T. (1995). Making sense of software: Computer games and interactive textuality. In S. G. Jones (Ed.), *CyberSociety: Computer-mediated communication and community* (pp. 73-89). Thousand Oaks, CA: Sage.

Friedson, E. (1953, June). Communication research and the concept of the mass. *American Sociological Review, 18*.

Frith, S. (1981). *Sound effects: Youth, leisure, and the politics of rock 'n' roll*. New York: Pantheon.

Fuller, M., & Jenkins, H. (1995). Nintendo and New World travel writing: A dialogue. In S. G. Jones (Ed.), *CyberSociety: Computer-mediated communication and community* (pp. 57-72). Thousand Oaks, CA: Sage.

Gans, H. (1974). *Popular culture and high culture: An analysis and evaluation of taste.* New York: Basic Books.

Gerbner, G. (1984). Liberal education in the information age. In *Current issues in higher education (1983-1984).* American Association for Higher Education. (Reprinted 1991 in A. A. Berger, Ed., *Media USA,* 2nd edition, New York: Longman)

Gitlin, T. (1989, July / August). Postmodernism defined, at last! *Utne Reader,* pp. 52-58, 61.

Gowans, A. (1981). *Learning to see: Historical perspectives on modern popular/commercial arts.* Bowling Green, OH: Bowling Green University Popular Press.

Graña, C. (1967). *Modernity and its discontents.* New York: Harper Torchbooks.

Henderson, J. L. (1968). Ancient myths and modern man. In C. G. Jung (Ed.), *Man and his symbols.* New York: Dell.

Hendin, H. (1975). *The age of sensation.* New York: W. W. Norton.

Heuscher, J. E. (1974). *A psychiatric study of myths and fairy tales.* Springfield, IL: Charles C Thomas.

Iser, W. (1988). The reading process: A phenomenological approach. In D. Lodge (Ed.), *Modern criticism and theory: A reader.* New York: Longman.

Jakobson, R. (1988). Linguistics and poetics. In D. Lodge (Ed.), *Modern criticism and theory: A reader* (pp. 32-57). New York: Longman.

Jameson, F. (1984). Postmodernism and the consumer society. In H. Foster (Ed.), *Postmodern culture.* London: Pluto.

Jung, C. G. (Ed.). (1968). *Man and his symbols.* New York: Dell.

Katz, E., Blumler, J. G., & Gurevitch, M. (1979). Utilization of mass communication by the individual. In G. Gumpert & R. Cathcart (Eds.), *Inter/media.* New York: Oxford University Press.

Kris, E. (1964). *Psychoanalytic explorations in art.* New York: Schocken.

Lakoff, G., & Johnson, M. (1980). *Metaphors we live by.* Chicago: University of Chicago Press.

Lazarsfeld, P. F., Berelson, B., & Gaudet, B. (1968). *The people's choice* (3rd ed.). New York: Columbia University Press. (Original work published 1944)

Le Bon, G. (1960). *The crowd: A study of the popular mind.* New York: Viking. (Original work published 1895)

Lévi-Strauss, C. (1967). *Structural anthropology.* Garden City, NY: Doubleday.

Lotman, J. M. (1977). *The structure of the artistic text* (G. Lenhoff & R. Vroon, Trans.). Ann Arbor: Michigan Slavic Contributions.

Lowenthal, L. (1944). Biographies in popular magazines. In P. F. Lazarsfeld & F. Stanton (Eds.), *Radio research 1942-43.* New York: Duell, Sloan & Pearce.

Lyotard, J.-F. (1984). *The postmodern condition: A report on knowledge.* Minneapolis: University of Minnesota Press.

McAnany, E. G. (1991). Wilbur Schramm: In memoriam. In A. A. Berger (Ed.), *Media USA* (2nd ed.). New York: Longman.

McBride, S., et al. (1980). *Many voices, one world* (report by the International Commission for the Study of Communication Problems). Paris/London: UNESCO/ Kegan Paul.

McCombs, M., & Shaw, D. L. (1976). Structuring the "unseen environment." *Journal of Communication, 26*(2).

McGuire, W. (1986). The myth of massive media impact: Savagings and salvagings. In G. Comstock (Ed.), *Public communication and behavior* (Vol. 1, pp. 173-257). Orlando, FL: Academic Press.

McGuire, W. (1988). Who's afraid of the big bad media? In A. A. Berger (Ed.), *Media USA*. New York: Longman.

McGuire, W. (1991). Who's afraid of the big bad media? In A. A. Berger (Ed.), *Media USA* (2nd ed.). New York: Longman.

McLuhan, M. (1951). *The mechanical bride: Folklore of industrial man*. Boston: Beacon.

McLuhan, M. (1965). *Understanding media: The extensions of man*. New York: McGraw-Hill.

McQuail, D. (1969). *Towards a sociology of mass communications*. London: Macmillan.

McQuail, D., & Windahl, S. (1993). *Communication models: For the study of mass communication* (2nd ed.). New York: Longman.

Messaris, P. (1994). *Visual literacy: Image, mind, and reality*. Boulder, CO: Westview.

Nisbet, R. (1976). *Sociology as an art form*. New York: Oxford University Press.

Noelle-Neumann, E. (1974). The spiral of silence: A theory of public opinion. *Journal of Communication, 24*(2), 43-51.

Parenti, M. J. (1986). *Inventing reality: The politics of the mass media*. New York: St. Martin's.

Pierce, J. R., & Noll, A. M. (1990). *Signals: The science of telecommunications*. New York: Scientific American Library.

Postman, N. (1986). *Amusing ourselves to death: Public discourse in the age of show business*. New York: Viking Penguin.

Powell, C. (1988). A phenomenological analysis of humor in society. In C. Powell & G. E. C. Paton (Eds.), *Humour in society: Resistance and control*. New York: St. Martin's.

Powell, C., & Paton, G. E. C. (Eds.). (1988). *Humour in society: Resistance and control*. New York: St. Martin's.

Propp, V. (1968). *The morphology of the folktale* (2nd ed.). Austin: University of Texas Press. (Original work published 1928)

Read, H. (1966). *Art and society*. New York: Schocken.

Reid, E. (1995). Virtual worlds: Culture and imagination. In S. G. Jones (Ed.), *Cyber-Society: Computer-mediated communication and community* (pp. 164-183). Thousand Oaks, CA: Sage.

Richie, D. (1969). *Rashomon* and Kurosawa. In D. Richie (Ed.), *Rashomon: A film by Akira Kurosawa*. New York: Grove.

Riley, J. W., & Riley, M. W. (1959). Mass communication and the social system. In R. K. Merton, L. Broom, & S. Cottrell (Eds.), *Sociology today*. New York: Basic Books.

Rosenberg, B. (1957). Mass culture in America. In B. Rosenberg & D. M. White (Eds.), *Mass culture: The popular arts in America*. New York: Free Press.

Sapir, E. (1929). The status of linguistics as a science. *Language, 5*.

Saussure, F. de. (1966). *A course in general linguistics* (W. Baskin, Trans.). New York: McGraw-Hill.

Schwartz, T. (1974). *The responsive chord*. Garden City, NY: Doubleday.

Schwartz, T. (1983). *Media: The second god*. Garden City, NY: Anchor.

Sholes, R. (1974). *Structuralism in literature: An introduction*. New Haven, CT: Yale University Press.

Siebert, F., Peterson, T., & Schramm, W. (1963). *Four theories of the press*. Urbana: University of Illinois Press.

Signorelli, N., & Gerbner, G. (1988). *Violence and terror in the mass media: An annotated bibliography*. Westport, CT: Greenwood.

Smythe, D. W., & Dinh, T. V. (1983). On critical and administrative research: A new critical analysis. *Journal of Communication, 33*(3).

Steiner, G. E. (1991). Radio: What once made it ours and ours alone. In A. A. Berger (Ed.), *Media USA* (2nd ed.). New York: Longman.

Stephenson, W. (1988). *The play theory of mass communication*. New Brunswick, NJ: Transaction. (Original work published 1967)

Sutton-Smith, B. (1988). Introduction to the Transaction edition. In W. Stephenson, *The play theory of mass communication*. New Brunswick, NJ: Transaction.

Thompson, M., Ellis, R., & Wildavsky, A. (1990). *Cultural theory*. Boulder, CO: Westview.

Tuchman, G. (1978). The symbolic annihilation of women by the mass media. In G. Tuchman, A. K. Daniels, & J. Benet (Eds.), *Hearth and home: Images of women in the mass media*. New York: Oxford University Press.

Wellek, R., & Warren, A. (1977). *Theory of literature* (3rd ed.). New York: Harcourt Brace Jovanovich.

Wildavsky, A. (1989). A cultural theory of preference formation. In A. A. Berger (Ed.), *Political culture and public opinion*. New Brunswick, NJ: Transaction.

Wollen, P. (1972). *Signs and meaning in the cinema*. Bloomington: Indiana University Press.

Zeman, J. J. (1977). Peirce's theory of signs. In T. A. Sebeok (Ed.), *A perfusion of signs*. Bloomington: Indiana University Press.

Zettl, H. (1990). *Sight-sound-motion: Applied media aesthetics* (2nd ed.). Belmont, CA: Wadsworth.

Zito, G. V. (1975). *Methodology and meaning: Varieties of sociological inquiry*. New York: Praeger.

NAME INDEX

SUBJECT INDEX

ABOUT THE AUTHOR

Arthur Asa Berger is a writer, artist, and self-styled secret agent, searching out hidden meanings and latent functions in popular culture and the mass media. He is Professor of Broadcast and Electronic Communication Arts at San Francisco State University, where he has taught since 1965. He is the author of numerous articles and books on popular culture and related concerns. Among his books are *Media Analysis Techniques* (revised edition, 1991), *Seeing Is Believing: An Introduction to Visual Communication* (1989), *An Anatomy of Humor* (1993), *Blind Men and Elephants: Perspectives on Humor* (1994), and *Cultural Criticism: A Primer of Key Concepts* (1995). He is film and television review editor for *Society* maga-

zine; editor of a series of reprints, "Classics in Communication"; and a consulting editor for *Humor* magazine. He has appeared on *20/20* and *The Today Show,* and appears frequently on various local radio and television programs in the San Francisco area. This is his seventh book for Sage Publications.